MY AWAKENING THROUGH LOVES, LOSSES AND LAUGHTER

Hugs and Mush, Gommy

BY SHIRLEY BRADY (GOMMY)

Copyright 2018 – Shirley Brady
CreateSpace Edition
ISBN-13: 978-1724727176
ISBN-10: 1724727176

Introduction

I wrote this book, in part, hoping that it may help others find the answers that we all ask about life. My book will take you through the many highs and lows of my life. It will also take you along on my spiritual quest to understand what I call 'The All That Is'- The ONE Creator.

I also hope that my story will help someone, anyone, who has ever experienced loss and may want or need to hear about my own experiences with loss. And that it may help them navigate through their own feelings of sadness and helplessness.

This is not a book on religion, but I will explain my thoughts on the Divine because my questions about religion are in part what led me to my spiritual path.

How many of you have ever wanted to know the real meaning of life? I will thread together the many life experiences that caused me to search for my own answers. And you may just recognize that some of your own questions are similar to the ones that started me on my search.

SPOILER ALERT: What I have discovered is that the true purpose of life is to wake up. To Awaken.

My book chronicles my recollection of my early years, and also how I managed to get through the many losses I suffered in my life. I explain how I've come to understand what this gift called Life is all about. And how I questioned myself, if all the labels that I had assigned to me, were really who I am.

I felt strongly that since I am not any more special than anyone else, that if I could sense the truths of what I was understanding, then anyone else could understand them as well. I found that it just takes asking, and the answers will come. At least they did for me. And I am not trying to change anyone else's beliefs, but by sharing mine, I hope that I may shed light on some of the questions that many of us share.

I explain that with the help of many spiritual teachers, scholars, and even scientists along the way, how it helped me understand my questions more clearly. And of course how the many prayers that I made along the way, asking for the guidance also allowed me to understand it all.

I hope you will enjoy going down memory lane with me, and also reading about my journey down The Yellow Brick Road to 'awakening.'

Dedication

To Terry, Tiffany, Mom, Dad, and all of my family and
loved ones who have already transitioned…..

I wish you were here!!

XOXO

Acknowledgments

Books usually have an acknowledgment page in them. It's a way to thank those who have contributed to what is written on the pages. I would have to say that my thanks, acknowledgments, and inspiration for writing this book must go in part to the highs and lows of my very own life, and to those who have shared it with me.

I have stumbled and even fallen at times in life, but without those painful experiences and the people who stood by me so that I could stand back up again, I would not have been able to look back at it all and see the gifts that came as a result of some of those stumbles.

I can't express enough how grateful I am for my husband Mike and my daughter Tracey. They are the reason that I want to live another day. I am also grateful for my late husband Terry and my late son and daughter Terry and Tiffany for the years that we shared. Nothing is as beautiful as the unconditional love of family. Now and in our past.

Saying thank you does not even begin to convey how much I appreciate everyone who has shown me great love, compassion, and support throughout my life. And although I am not one to easily display my feelings of affection, I must say a very heartfelt thank you from the bottom of my heart to all who have shared my journey with me. I will be eternally grateful to you. The names are too long to list, and I wouldn't want to leave anyone out….but I do hope you know who you are!

I would also like to thank someone that I've never met in person. Stacey Brown. My granddaughter Megan's mother-in-law, another Stacy, turned me onto a friend of hers who is also an author. Stacey Brown helped me when she didn't really have to take the time. But she did take the time and she generously answered my numerous questions about self-publishing. And she also pushed me to 'pull the trigger' when I was feeling iffy, OK......petrified, about putting this book out for the public to read. So thank you very, very much Stacey. I truly appreciate your help. And I hope we get the chance to meet one day. And thank you to Stacy Troy as well for leading me to Stacey! You both ROCK!

Oh, and the Hugs and Mush part of the title? I have to give credit to my daughter Tiffany for that. It's how Tiffany always signed off when she wrote a note or a letter to anyone. So thanks Spiffy Tiffy for continuing to be a huge part of my journey.

Table of Contents

CHAPTER 1

So You Want to Write a Book?

So, why did I decide to write a book you might ask? Well, I had posted a comment in the "What's on your mind" option on Facebook about a time in my life that I was reminiscing about. I received quite a lot of comment replies and 'Likes' back saying that I should write a book. So, I half-heartedly replied that maybe I just might.

How many times have you heard someone say, "I could write a book!"? Well, I have too. So then I thought that maybe someone, anyone, somewhere, may just be interested in what I have learned along the way.

And at the age that I find myself to be right now, if I wanted to still be alive so I could know if you liked it,– I figured that I had better get going on it - - and fast!

I've had many other people tell me on occasion that I should put my thoughts down in a book. But you know how it is - - you don't think anyone would actually care to read about your life. But the more I thought about it, the more I realized that I have had a pretty remarkable life. And as one friend said to me, "Even if nothing ever comes of it, at least my daughter and my grandchildren will have a chronicle of their ol' Goms' life".

I've also heard that writing about one's life is cathartic. And who couldn't use a little self-imposed therapy? *raises hand*

I found that re-living my life in words was liberating at least, and healing at best. You see, there have been some preeeeety sad times in my life. But there have also been some very wonderful times that I am blessed to be able to reminisce about, and now share with all of you.

I found as I was writing down my memories, the puzzle pieces of my life seemed to be fitting together in ways that allowed me to see more clearly how and why certain people came into my life, how others went out of my life, and what I had learned from each encounter. And to see the lessons offered in these encounters. Lessons that I didn't always recognize as being lessons at the time.

As you read my story, you will notice that I prefer to accentuate my blessings, rather than dwell for very long on the sad times of my life. But all of my life experiences make up the whole of my journey so I will share the good times, and the bad times, and in the in-between times as well. And I feel that shedding light on the dark times can help us to understand them more clearly.

As the saying goes, a single candle can define as well as defy the darkness. It can help others to see from a different perspective as well. And I'm all about helping others whenever I can. It's a shame that more people can't do this. Or that they can't be happy for other people. But I have learned that this is because they just haven't found their own happiness yet.

The quote that comes to mind is, 'Comparison is the thief of joy'. And if you take the time to understand what this quote means, you may have a little awakening right here and now your own self. Oops….I just snuck in a little bit of my Woo-Woo-ness there. But there's lots more woo-woo later on, but I don't want to scare you away just yet. So, just stay with me Peeps, and maybe you will get some useful nuggets from my story that may help you too…..that is if you are able to keep an open mind.

Another reason I chose to write my thoughts down was that I felt it would be a real waste to take all of this hard-earned knowledge that I have accumulated with me to the grave and not share it.

My hope is that it may help those who may be going through similar experiences, to hear my journey and how I navigated through them. And if my life can be used to shine a light on their path…..then the time allotted to me in Earth School has been worthwhile. So here we go Peeps, ready or not.

CHAPTER 2

Oh I'm fine, how about you?

We never really know what people have gone through in their life. But we all do have our ups and downs. And I sure have had my share as well. As you read my story, you will see that my downs have REALLY, REALLY been down there in the depths of unimaginable sorrow, pain, and grief.

However, I do think that the 'dark night of the soul' times that I've experienced have made me appreciate my 'ups' much more than I ever would or could have if I hadn't experienced such fierce, sorrowful, and dramatic lows. Life IS all about contrasts after all.

Dark Night of the Soul refers to when we suffer "a period of spiritual desolation, in which all sense of consolation is removed." It's when we lose faith in everything that we thought we ever knew.

When you parse them all out, you will see that I've actually had many different and varied lives. Not counting the ones that I've had before this one. (Yeah, I know…another woo-woo clue. But be patient, there's lots more to follow).

So, about my years here on Earth School, (as the author and spiritual teacher Gary Zukav refers to our physical time on Earth). There were the early years growing up as an only child. There were the years during my K-12 schooling. The years after graduating from high school and getting my cosmetologist license. There were the working years before marrying at the tender age of 19. There were the years when I was a young mother of 3 beautiful children, all by the age of 26. And then the young adult years of raising a family.

Then there were the years of too much tragedy for anyone to imagine, never mind having to live through. Then the empty nest years. And I can't forget the years of successes and failures that were mingled in between. And finally, the years that I am living now, with who knows what is in store for my 'final chapter' years. Pun intended.

As I look back, I can see how I never allowed my emotions to surface when I was a child. I now understand that it was because my Mom was a tough cookie herself and had always told me to keep my chin up, have a stiff upper lip, not to whine, and to never make a scene. And this is not a slam to my Mom at all, because she only taught me from her own level of understanding and consciousness at the time.

But I see now, how we can be molded into personalities that do not always portray our core essence. For a while anyway. But we can and do come back to our core as life unfolds for us. It's like the big beach ball that we try to keep under water. Eventually, it pops up when you 'let go'. And it can pop up at very inappropriate times.

I find myself able to cry much more easily as I have grown older. But it was a process. An un-peeling of sorts. Now when I feel tears well up and get that tightness in my chest when something sentimental comes up in life, or on TV, or at the movies, I have to admit that I welcome those emotions. And I don't feel uncomfortable or confused anymore when they do arise. I feel cleansed and lighter.

When the world seems to be spinning much too quickly for my comfort level these days, and I'm not feeling quite in love with what is happening around me, I know how to slow it down, just by closing my eyes and breathing deeply and not allowing myself to get caught up in the whirlwind of life. And I can also observe the monkey-talk that is always going on in our heads, and choose not to listen to it.

They say you should make every day count so that when our final moment comes and our life flashes before our eyes – we are able to smile, enjoy the 'show', and be pleased with the images that we see of how our life played out. And I sure am doing my very best to make sure that my 'production' going forward is epic and is something that I will greatly enjoy!

CHAPTER 3

Is that another shoe I hear dropping?

I'm pleased to say that many of my years can be described as very, very 'up' years. I have had many happy and incredibly blessed years to look back on.

But then there are also the very, very sad years, such as when my husband Terry was just 34 years old, and he died suddenly in a car accident. Our children were 8, 11 and 12 at the time, and I was 34 as well.

As one can imagine, this was most definitely a very low and understandably heartbreaking time in our lives to say the very least. Then 9 years later, two of my three beautiful children were killed in another car accident. This was another desperately low and tragically sad time in our life.

Losing a husband is a very, very sad thing for sure, but losing children is an unthinkable tragedy of great sadness and proportion. More than you could ever imagine. Nor would you want to. We are not meant to outlive our children. It just isn't natural.

I had naively thought that we had experienced all of the tragedy that would befall us as a family when my husband died so young. But nooooooo, it turned out that life had a lot more trials, tribulations, and sadness for our family to maneuver in, around, and eventually through.

I can now fully understand the saying that you don't know how strong you are until you have no choice. No one in their right mind would want to experience such sadness, but when it does happen in your life, you have two choices: You have to make the decision if you want to go on....or to check out. And at the time, I felt as if I had checked into The Hotel California, and there was no way to ever leave.

As depressing as it is, we must recognize that none of us gets 'out of here' without some sadness and losses in our lives. Some of us get our sadness meted out over the years, and some get it all at once. And it may seem that some people are escaping any sadness in their lives at all. But no, even they will find that they will have their sad times too; and it may come at the end of their lives. But I know now that 'acceptance' is what will finally get you through these sad times.

And I want to be clear here that acceptance is not at all the same thing as 'liking' when something happens. I will explain this more when I get into the spiritual part of my journey.

I really don't know in which part of our life that it's worse to face a tragedy. For me, burying my husband and then my children were my 'worst'. And those sad times came when I was very young. But losing any loved one, no matter our age or their age brings us great suffering and is very, very heartbreaking, as well as life-changing.

Our family dynamic and our definition of life are never the same after losing a loved one. PERIOD. Life after a loss is forever divided into before the loss and after the loss.

I do think the people who sail through life, with everything going so smoothly for them and then BAM, they are faced with the horrible pain and suffering of sickness or worse – losing a loved one, may just have a harder time of coping with what is facing them. I don't think that they are as equipped to handle it as those who were young when the 'dark night of the soul' came knocking on their door. I suspect that this is because they had lived a long time without loss ever touching them. But as I said, no one 'gets out' of this life experience without having to face some sadness. And I know this for certain.

And then there are those who we may think never seem to have any tough times in their lives at all. But the truth is that we really don't know what goes on behind the 'highlight reels' that they project and offer to the outside world. Some of the saddest among us put on a brave front each day, and we never know what they are really feeling deep inside. They can often feel lonely in a world full of people. I have found that there is no amount of money that can buy the feeling of belonging.

Most people experience an 'everyday' kind of reality in their life. And they may feel that there are those who are apparently living it up and don't have a care in the world. But some of those very people have problems that you would never swap for any that you may have. And you would probably be shocked to find that in some instances, they would gladly trade places and any material things that they have, for the meaningful relationship you share with your spouse. So, don't judge a book by its cover, as the saying goes. (I'm kinda loving these book puns – Ha!).

Thinking back, I can see that I had always come from a place of always being told what to do by my Mom for 19 years, and then by my late husband Terry for the next 15 years. I'm not blaming them for my own submissiveness. I guess I was just a 'go with the flow' kinda girl who didn't like to make waves. And I still don't like confrontations. You would think that I would have been able to overcome that side of my personality by the time I had reached the ripe old.....errr.....mature age that I am now. But some aspects of our persona are so ingrained in us, that even age can't erase some of our feelings of uneasiness.

On the surface, I guess that I could have been perceived as being a tad stoic and unfeeling by some who didn't know me well. But inside, I was just trying to not make waves. And the way that I always dealt with that, was not to interject my opinion very often about the happenings around me. I later discovered that the 'ostrich head in the sand' approach to life can get you into trouble. A WHOLE LOTTA TROUBLE I tell ya'.

After my husband died, people began asking me what I wanted to do about this or that, and I would actually look behind me to see who they were talking to. No one had ever considered asking me about things before or even asked for my opinion.

Of course I was in charge of raising our children, and in my opinion, that was more important than anything else I could have ever done. And more rewarding too. But the everyday big decisions in our lives were handled by my husband. And after his death, I quickly realized that I had to toughen up pretty quickly or be taken advantage of.

And taken advantage of I was! And it was by some of my husband's 'friends'. One guy came and took his bulldozer and said he would sell it for me. He didn't. He kept it for himself. Geesh, right?

Another situation where I was taken advantage of was by the gas station owner in our little town. A handshake kind of deal had been made between them, that Terry would clear the owner of the gas station's property with our bulldozer for him, in trade for gas and other fuel that Terry used in his other equipment.

Well, guess what? After Terry died, I was sent a large bill for said gas and fuel! GEESH again, right? But I didn't have a leg to stand on because Terry was 'old school' – and he considered his handshake was his bond. No contract? Pay up Sistah! Sadly, the gas station owner didn't appear to possess the same integrity as Terry.

Others helped themselves to Terry's tools, of which there were many and very expensive. Even the government took advantage of my ignorance of not knowing what was going on. It looked like my head needed to be coming out of the sand in a hurry- - ready or not!

There had been an ongoing IRS audit for our business when my husband died. This is one of the times where the 'ostrich approach' bit me in the arse. Big Time!

My husband was self-employed at the time of his accident, and we had an office in our home. He had the usual office expenses and other travel related expenditures that are notorious as 'red flags' to the IRS. These items raise questions about people trying to hide wages, padding allowable expenses, etc. And those red flag items were what Terry was trying to prove to the IRS as actual and legitimate expenses. And they were. I may not have been involved in Terry's business but I did know that he used our home office to conduct his business. There were long distance phone call expenses (there were no cell phones with unlimited plans back then), and the office supplies, airplane and hotel travel expenses, etc. They were all very real business expenses!

I didn't have detailed knowledge of all of the intricacies of my husband's business, so when Terry died, the IRS froze all of our assets. Even our bank accounts. I remember going to the IRS office and being very, very scared.

Back in those days the IRS promoted and was proud of their reputation of scaring people so that we taxpayers wouldn't even think of cheating on our income taxes. I remember going to the very sparsely decorated IRS office and being frightened to pieces. I recall that it had a red, white and blue theme running throughout the entire office and in all of the cubicles as well. Of course it did!

They said that I owed them a lot of money, and at that point, I really didn't know what to do. It's a very scary thing to be the little 'gal' going up against the big, badass IRS.

We had our home and acreage that we lived on, and we also had some investment property on the Caloosahatchee River that Terry had been clearing building lots for, and had planned to build and develop home sites on. He worked on the river property when he was in town and wasn't traveling for his other business.

I tried to explain to the IRS that the river property had a great deal of value and would be more than ample to pay any amount that they said I owed for taxes. But they were firm about wanting to take all of our possessions first, and then see if anything was left over for us after the fines, penalties, and interest were paid. YIKES….and GULP!

I eventually had to secure a tax attorney and he 'persuaded' the IRS to swap any taxes they felt that I owed, along with any fees and fines, for our river property. I think the IRS made out better than the children and I did. And so did the tax attorney I think. But at least they removed the freeze on my bank account and I didn't have to continue getting food stamps for us to survive on.

It gave me a very bitter taste in my mouth to think they would take advantage of a young widow with 3 young children, especially when I had heard of several businessmen who were forgiven millions and millions of dollars that they owed for their taxes. But we persevered and moved on with what was left of our lives. Although I have to admit that it was a very frightening time for me.

As I look back on those days it reminds me of the saying that it doesn't matter how many times you are knocked down as long as you keep getting back up!

It also caused me to feel great empathy for, and have a different perspective on how people who have to depend on food stamps to survive may feel. Everyone on assistance isn't on it because they want to be. Believe me! I never judge anyone when I see them using their WIC stamps or cards at the store.

I remember all too vividly the time that I had to use them to feed my own family. And I never begrudge paying my taxes, knowing that some of that money is used to help people in need. I am very grateful that assistance was available to us when we so desperately needed the help.

The irony meter was off the charts when you think that on the one hand, the government was raking us over the coals and leaving us with nothing to live on, and on the other hand, they were giving us food stamps so that we could eat. Contrasts again!

Maybe going through what we did all those years ago, helped to make me the proud Snowflake that I am today. (Snowflake being the term meant as an insult in politics)

I tried to hide how sad and afraid I was from the children. I worried that they would be even more frightened if they thought that I was falling apart too. They had experienced enough in their little lives to handle, without a Mom who was a basket case.

But later, my daughter told me that she thought at the time that it seemed as if I didn't care deeply enough that her Dad had died. I would have done things a lot differently if I had the chance to go back and do it all over again. It showed me that people's perspectives can be skewed by how we present or hide our feelings; and that what we perceive isn't always what is actually going on or being felt by another person. Perspective is something you gain the longer you live and experience life.

After a time, I guess the 'power' of making my own decisions must have gone to my head because I balked at anyone telling me anything for a while. If someone even said have a nice day – I felt like saying, "Don't tell me what to do!"

I went from being a bit too submissive and naive to acting as if I was a hammer and everyone else was a nail. I eventually figured out that that wasn't who I really was in my core essence, and it just didn't feel good to be behaving that way. So I eased up and became my more temperate 'me' again.

My beautiful and compassionate daughter Tracey was part of the reason that I dialed it back too. She would tell me to bring it down a notch and pump the brakes when I was over-reacting. Our children are our greatest teachers at times.

CHAPTER 4

Second Act?

In between becoming a young widow and Terry and Tiffany's accident, I met and married the man that I am still married to today. And I will be until I am no longer on this Earth. I always refer to Mike as my LAST husband. He never does laugh when I say that though. LOL. But I do mean it. I would never marry again because I don't think I could ever be lucky enough to find a man who could be my husband AND my best friend, as Mike is to me. That's assuming I outlive him of course - and I have already told him that I would gladly go first because I can't imagine my life without him in it.

Mike is the most kind, giving, honest, outgoing, optimistic and friendly people-loving person you will ever have the honor of knowing. He is so generous that I always joke that he'd give you the shirt off MY back as well as his.

He came into my life at a time that I needed to know that life could go on. But my children were having a very hard adjustment after losing their father. They were also having a hard time handling the move from their beloved country home back to the city.

We soon found that blended families can either make or break a relationship. And it did push Mike's and my relationship over the brink for a time. But we did figure it out eventually, and we made it back to each other because we loved each other too much to stay apart. And I want to make it clear that whatever blended family problems that we had, were no fault of anyone in particular. It was just that it took us a while to figure it all out.

But I have to say that I've been very blessed to have had two incredible men choose me to marry them. You could say that I won the marriage lottery twice!

I also discovered that you can love two different men in a lifetime. And each man can have very different personalities from each other. So the theory that we have only one soulmate didn't turn out to be true for me.

Both of my husband's hearts were/are bigger than life itself. Both always gave generously to others and helped whenever they saw a need. They both had/have great friendships with many wonderful people of all ages. They are both loved greatly by most anyone whose paths they have crossed. And they both have personality traits that anyone would value in a husband or friend; great character, generosity, integrity, and honesty.

Both of my husbands were great teachers for me as well. They taught me how to be more generous, and that good character is a trait that we should always strive to achieve. I love the comparison between character and reputation. It's that your character is much more important than your reputation. Your character is who you really are and your reputation is 'only' what others think of you. And both Terry and Mike are the epitome of integrity and good character.

Another lucky thing for me is that both of my husbands were born in September, making them Virgos. I am a Virgo as well, and they say that only Virgos can stand to live with another Virgo because they are such perfectionists. But as a wife, you couldn't get a better husband than a Virgo, precisely BECAUSE they are so tidy and neat in their perfectionism. I've never had to pick up after either of my husbands. They've always put their stuff away and they never left wet towels or clothes on the floor. So take that into consideration when you are looking for a mate ladies! It is a gift from the stars, I promise.

I feel that everyone we meet in life teaches us lessons that we are here to learn. Both of my husband's taught me that being generous doesn't take anything away from your own life, and the more generous you are, actually fills your life back up even more abundantly!

Both of my husbands came from large families. Terry was the second of five, and Mike is the fifth of seven.

In Terry's family, there was Tom (always known as OUR Tommy), Terry, Gail, Tim, and Melody. Sadly, Terry and Melody have now passed.

Mike's family are all still with us. There is Bridget, Cathy, Bubba, Susan, Mike, Leo, and Colleen.

Coming from a large family can mold you into becoming who you will be to some degree. Of course, this depends on your core personality and how you see life to begin with. And family can have helpful and unhelpful dynamics.

I have come to understand how our 'personal reality' can be formed in part by our family. Gary Zukav explains (paraphrased), [When individual souls come together, they form a group energy field. Sort of a merger of the soul energy of all in the group. Therefore, the decisions that you make within your personal reality, such as the decision to be giving or to be selfish, or the decision to be angry or to be understanding, contribute to the shaping of the reality that you share with your family. Your father's dependability or drunkenness, or your mother's timid or assertive nature, also contributes to the level of your own reality. As does your sibling's jealousy or support of you, and yours of them].

I have also noticed that many of us choose to either be very much like our parents or to be very unlike them. This depends on what sort of relationship that we did have within our own particular family. And I have also read, that on some level, we choose our mates to heal a relationship that we had or didn't have with our own parent(s). Hmmmmmm...... think about that for a minute!

My late husband Terry was a very compassionate and loving person, who I don't believe ever fully recognized his own self-worth. And that is a sad thing for me to come to terms with, now that he is gone. He felt things so deeply, and he didn't understand how others could not feel as passionately about some things as he did. Even in his own family.

But even members of the same family don't always possess the same behaviors or viewpoints. Many times we find siblings being the complete opposite of the others. Some members of the same family can be compassionate and kind, while others can be pompous, cold, know it all's! I love the quote that says, "How come know-it-alls don't know how annoying they are?" Good one right?

Terry would have loved it if all of our family, on both sides, could have lived in a commune on the 'farm' with us. Both Terry and Mike were/are never happier than when spending time with family.

Mike and I often watch the Hallmark Channel, and by the end of the movie, we are both crying. Most of the movies touch on family in some fashion, and that gets to us both. But we are always grateful that they all have happy endings.

Terry experienced life on a much deeper level than most people do. When he would drink sometimes, I know that it was to numb some of those feelings that he didn't know what to do with. But that never does work. I wish I would have been able to help him through some of those feelings he was having, the way I know I could now. But I had a hard time even showing or dealing with my own feelings back then; so I wasn't able to.

I know now that pushing down our feelings is not a substitute for working them out or at least talking them out. And that holding feelings in is rather like an incubator that breeds even more troublesome emotions.

We all have things that we use to dull the feelings that we don't know what to do with. Some use food. Some use alcohol. Some use gambling. Some use drugs. And some people use their personalities, by being bullies, who feel they have to make others look small so that they can feel 'big'- because deep down, they actually feel inadequate themselves.

I would have loved it if I had been able to let Terry know how much more attractive he was in being a little self-effacing than to be the boorish, brash, pompous asses that some people are.

There are many other things that we humans do to make us feel that we matter or to feel that we are enough and that we measure up to what we think would make us more respected or valued in other people's eyes.

But all of these 'crutches' are merely ways in which we are looking to 'tame' the self-doubts that we have about ourselves and our lives.

Knowing what I do about life now, I could have shared with Terry that everyone responds and reacts differently and that while they don't show their emotions or affection in the same way that we may, it doesn't always mean that they don't care. But I was not 'awake' enough at that time to have helped Terry. That is a regret that I will always carry. But I also remind myself that we all do choose the life that we 'drop into'. And then I ask myself, who am I to judge that everything didn't turn out exactly as it was supposed to? I suppose I will know the why's more clearly when we meet again one day. (More explanation on the 'drop-in' part a little later).

Mike, on the other hand, has always been supremely self-confident, and his family dynamic didn't affect him in the way that Terry's did. That is because Mike has always been self-assured. And although Mike is also very compassionate and extremely generous, and feels deeply about things, the opinions that others have of him didn't have the same influence or power over him.

As I look back, I know that I was a good wife to Terry, but I will always wish that I could have helped him more with the feelings he was having back then. But, we grow as we learn and that's just the way it is. As Maya Angelou said, "When we know better, we do better".

Being 'awake' has allowed me to be a better wife to Mike than I ever was to Terry. I love both men, but it turns out that both men got a very different version of me as a wife and companion.

We can also be better human beings by remembering that we can never be prettier by acting ugly. We can never be richer by making someone else poorer. And we can never be made more important by trying to make someone else look less than.

I am so very grateful for the many people in my life who have taught me these things along the way. Some people who have tried to hurt me, don't even realize how much they have taught me and helped me. I am possibly even more grateful to them because they have shown me who I don't want to be like.

I believe there is a lesson in every encounter, person, and experience that we have on our Storyboard Journey. If you look for the lessons and be very honest with yourself, you will grow as a person and your understanding will expand as well. And that is also what everyone is trying to attain in life. Or should be at least.

Sometimes we are the teacher and sometimes we are the student. But at all times.....we are learning life lessons - - if we pay attention.

CHAPTER 5

The Early Years

I suppose now would be a good place to explain my beginnings – before I became Gommy. Gommy being a mix of Grandma and Mommy.

I was born in Detroit, Michigan in 1948 to Kathleen and Guy Recchia. My father was born in 1896 and was an immigrant from Italy when he came over to the USA in the early 1900's. His name in Italian is Gaetano. Dad voyaged over to the United States when he was just 16 years old. His ticket for the voyage was in the steerage compartment of a steamship.

Dad had been a sheepherder back in Italy. Hey, my Dad was a shepherd! How many people can say that? And he came all the way over here to America, all by himself when he was really just a child by today's standards! His mission was to get to that enchanted land that he'd heard all about, where magical things were promised and dreams could come true.

Steerage refers to the section of the ship where 2nd class passengers were 'accommodated'. The name originates from the steering tackle, which runs through the bottom of the ship to connect the rudder to the tiller or the helm. The operative word here is 'bottom', as in the bottom of the ship – the VERY bottom.

If you Google 'steerage', it says, "Steerage was enormously profitable for steamship companies. Even though the average cost of a ticket back then was only $30, large ships could hold from 1,500 to 2,000 immigrants, netting a profit of $45,000 to $60,000 for a single, one-way voyage. The cost to feed a single immigrant was only about 60-cents a day!"

Amazing, right? I wonder what they served them. But as you might imagine, $45-60 thousand dollars was a lot of moolah back in those days, so it was quite a profitable business venture for the ships.

The voyage took about 6 weeks to make it across and with those travel conditions, you can suppose that my father didn't experience a very luxurious crossing to the USA. But I'm sure glad that he did or else I wouldn't be here myself!

Dad eventually found his way to Pueblo, Colorado because he had a family friend from the 'old country' that had come on ahead and had settled there. Dad worked in a coal mine there at first, and he told me how his mule, that he used in the coal mine, had the stereotypical attitude of the stubborn animal with a mind of its own. Dad told me that mules were considered more important than people because mules were needed to carry the coal out of the underground mines.

Dad said a good mule was a very valued and prized possession in that industry. And one can surely understand why that would be the case. No coal? No pay.

After a while, he decided to look for more pleasant conditions to work under, so he applied to work at a nickel-plating company that dipped typewriter keys in liquid nickel. (Google what a typewriter is for any of you young'uns who may be reading this).

The funny part of his story is that he didn't know what the heck nickel-plating was in the least. But when they asked him if he knew how to dip the keys in the nickel solution, he told them, in his very broken English, that he did. He said he just watched what the other workers did and it didn't seem too difficult, so his supervisors were never the wiser that they had hired a newbie who had never done that job before in his life.

It turns out that an Italian inventor named Pellegrino Turri invented the typewriter in 1808. He also invented carbon paper to provide the ink for his machine. And in 1823, Italina Pietro conti di Citavegna invented a new model of typewriter, the Tachigrafo, also known as Tachitipo. So, it all makes perfect sense to me that my very Italian Dad would end up working with typewriters sometime along his life journey! LOL

My Dad was a very brilliant man. And I'm not saying that just because he was my Dad. Dad taught himself the English language all by himself.

By the time I came along, he hardly spoke in broken English at all. Dad was 52 when I was born, and Mom was 30.

Dad was a very quiet man and he read vociferously. And not just 'dime-store novels'. He read Aristotle, Socrates, Plato, the Inquisition of Spain, and many history books.....and that was just for fun!

My Mom loved to read as a young girl too. She told me that she would go to the library to check out books, and would read 3 or 4 books a week! She passed that down to my little Grands because my granddaughter Samantha and grandson Brandon love reading too. And that makes me so happy. And I know their Great Grandma Katie is smiling down on them from wherever she is. It seems like many of the kids today just want to play video games, or play on their smartphones, or on the internet all day.

I'm not saying that Sam and Bran don't like to do those things too, but my daughter Tracey and son-in-law John, limit the time that they can play games on their iPads. And they monitor what they can see on them as well. And neither has a cell phone....yet. Tracey and John are really great parents. And again, I'm not just saying that because they are related to me.

They truly put everything they have into parenting their children. And believe me, it shows! Sam and Brandon are polite, studious, caring and thoughtful, kind children. Tracey makes sure that they HAND WRITE thank you notes for the gifts they receive too. What a concept, eh? Actually acknowledging when someone gives you something. Hmmmmmm!

My Dad had the most beautiful handwriting that you've ever seen. Except for his own father's handwriting, which was incredibly beautiful too. Dad had kept a letter from his father and when he showed it to me, I thought it was so perfect that it was hard to believe that it was done by someone's hand.

Dad would practice his cursive writing by drawing circles that looked like a long coil when he was finished. It was very important to him that his handwriting be perfect. On the other hand, I write like a chicken scratches. I'm sure it was the bane of my father's parenting of me.

Dad was also very artistic. A gene that regrettably he did not pass on to me either. But it did skip generations, as my daughter Tiffany was very artistic, as is my granddaughter Samantha and my grandson Terry. My grandson Brandon got the building and engineering gene from his very successful Daddy. My late husband, Brandon's granddad Terry, was a builder, plumber and very good at fixing anything too! Tracey's granddad Tom on her Dad's side, was a builder and could erect, build or remodel anything he put his mind to. And their Great Granddad Andy was a commercial artist. It's just in the genes I tell ya'.

Can you tell that I am over the moon in love with my little grands? Yeah, I thought so. It's one of my favorite oxymoron's = little grands. But more about them a little later. Uhhhhh, maybe even more than you care to hear. But that's what Gommy's are known to do – brag, brag, brag. Ha!

One of the very best things about Little Grands is that they still think you 'hung the moon' and they don't mind your wrinkles or other flaws that you may have. Because they just love you. Unconditionally. Period.

Oh, they do notice some things about your aging though, and they are not one bit shy about mentioning them. And they are always honest to a fault. But not in a judgmental way at all. Like how your gums have receded and the space between your gums and your crowns is now noticeable. And that chin hair that grows wild because you can't see it without full-blown sunlight and a mirror. Yep, those young eyes can spot that hair from 20 feet away! But they still love you in spite of your advancing years, your slower gait, and all the other 'wonders' that come with getting old.

There is a special kinship between Grands and Grandparents. I remember hearing it said that grandchildren and their grandparents have a common enemy - the parents! LOL. But they're not really enemies. Although Grandparents usually do allow the little grands to do whatever it is that they like to do. And they stick together and always have each other's backs! Of course, the little grands are not our responsibility, so it's much easier to be lenient with them, the way we never were with our own children. Point taken parents everywhere!

But back to my story now. I remember when I was about 8 years old, Dad said that maybe he would like to start drawing. I flippantly remarked that the only thing he could draw was flies. He didn't get angry or take offense, he just went to the store and bought some art supplies and began to draw, and then later to paint.

He loved it and he was pretty good at it too. He had always literally written on, colored on, drawn on, and painted on anything that was in front of him. One day, my Mom came home from work and Dad had painted a faux brick wall on our living room entryway. He even put a likeness of me doing a cartwheel in one of the bricks. Mom was not amused. But the 'mural' stayed. Probably because Mom didn't want to be the one to paint over it and Dad just wouldn't. Ha!

Dad had married a woman named Virginia years before he met and married my mother. Dad and Virginia had a son named David. Dad and Virginia divorced after David had sadly died around the age of 19 of carbon monoxide poisoning from working on his car in a closed garage.

I met Virginia at my Aunt Susie and Uncle Pete's (Dad's brother and sister-in-law) one time when she was visiting them. I was only around 8 or 9 at the time and I remember looking at Virginia with the 'stink-eye' because I didn't like the thought of her ever being married to MY Daddy.

Dad never talked much about David except to tell me that he had died unnecessarily because David's grandmother (Virginia's mother) had asked him to close the garage door because he was making too much noise working on his car. I guess the tragedy of losing their son was too much for the marriage between Dad and Virginia to survive. I eventually came to have a very different opinion of Virginia after I experienced the pain of losing a child myself. I'm sure she was a very nice woman, and I was just a kid who didn't have very much perspective on life at the time.

Dad kept an old-timey sepia photo of David in a book that was always on the end table by his chair in our living room. I do remember that Virginia was a pretty woman with red hair. My Dad was a looker himself, who was apparently very attractive to many ladies, as the story goes. My Daddy was a Ladies Man? Ewwwwww. We never do like to think of our parents that way, do we? But we should be grateful that our parents were sexual at least one time, or we wouldn't have been born.

I do remember that after a few glasses of good ol' Chianti, Dad could become uncharacteristically very loving and showed PDA, which was very unlike the more stoic Dad that I was used to seeing. Never too much as to be obnoxious. Just sweet and all lovey-dovey and huggy-huggy.

I remember my Mom telling me that women used to call my Dad, even after he and Mom were married. He kept a 'collection of his ladies' pictures in his wallet. That is until Mom found them and they mysteriously disappeared. The pictures….not the ladies. At least I don't know of any women who mysteriously disappeared. *wink*

While Dad was married to Virginia, he and his father-in-law got into a little business together. Turns out the business was illegal. Prohibition was in full force at the time and Dad and his business partner/father-in-law had a speak-easy (an illegal bar that served liquor) in their basement. They thought they were smarter than the average bear, i.e. Fed - and filled up some fake wall pipes with liquor to serve to their customers. It turned out that the Feds were a little smarter than they were, and put them both in the hoosegow, i.e. pokey, i.e. jail. I don't know how long they were in for, but Dad did say that he caught the crabs while he was in prison. Ewwww and YUCK!

After Dad and Virginia divorced, he moved to Detroit because his brother, Uncle Pete (Pietro), had come over from the old country by then too. They both ended up being cement contractors. What else would these two Italian brothers in the Midwest become, right?

Many Italians became brick masons and cement workers back then. Or they opened restaurants. But the only thing Italian that my Dad ever cooked was Pasta e Fagioli. In fact, one time when Mom and I were away, Terry stayed with Dad at our house and Terry said my Dad served him Pasta e Fagioli EVERY DAY for a week! Too funny.

Dad was never a slacker when it came to working and he always provided for our little family very well. It was always just Mom, Dad and me. No siblings for me. But Mom made sure I wasn't one of those spoiled 'only-children' types. I'll explain later.

Mom was born in Canada. The family came to America when my Grandma Maudie and Grandpa Bickley moved from Toronto, to just over the Detroit River. My Grandpa Bick was originally from Chicago and had moved to Detroit at some point. Since Grandpa was born in the USA, it allowed for his wife and children to become Naturalized American Citizens.

My Dad became an American Citizen as well sometime along the way. I remember him telling me that just before WWII began, Benito Mussolini had chosen to ally Italy's forces with those of Adolf Hitler. So the American government notified Dad that he had to come in and talk to them. They asked him who he would support if a war broke out – Italy or the U.S.A. Of course, he said he would defend the U.S.A., so they didn't put him in any sort of internment camp like was done to Japanese people after Pearl Harbor was attacked.

Grandma Maudie came over as a steerage passenger as well from Ireland when she was just 12 years old. Her mother had died, so her father shipped her and her brother off to live with his sister in Canada. Grandma said her Aunt was not very nice to them and they had to find a way to 'earn their keep' if they were to stay there. WOW, some Aunt, right????!! Sounds like a scene out of Oliver Twist.

To look older than she was, Grandma Maudie put her hair in a bun on top of her head and applied for a salesperson position at Eaton's Department store. At the time, Eaton's was Canada's largest department store. They hired her, not knowing she was so young. She told me how they didn't have electric registers back in the day, so they would use cash carriers, (pneumatic tubes that were like a zip line thingy) that carried customers' payments from the sales assistant to the cashier and carried the change and receipt back again to the customer.

Grandma Maudie met Grandpa 'Bick' and they fell in love at some point while they both lived in Canada. I don't know how they met and I sure do wish Grandma Maudie had told me, so I would know now. The only problem with their falling in love, and it was a big one back then, is that Grandpa was Catholic and Grandma was an Orangemen (Protestant).

Grandma told me of a time that a Catholic Priest, wearing a long black robe, came to her door to inform her that my mother (her new little baby girl) was a bastard because Grandma and Grandpa weren't married in the Catholic Church.

I had never heard my Grandma say a swear word in all the time that I knew her, but she could get her Irish dander up when she was angry. And as you can imagine, calling her sweet little baby girl a bastard just might do the trick in upsetting her..... just a wee tad!

Grandma Maudie said she chased the priest down the front steps with a broom, and all the way down the street, with him in his 'black skirt', and all the while yelling at him to never darken their door again. To say the least, she did not get along very well with Grandpa's side of the family.

I remember that Grandma always wore a 'housedress' and an apron around the house every day. Gram LOVED to shop and was always ready to go to the stores. She would joke and say, "Let me get me undies on and I'll be ready in a jif". She had very thinning hair and would always joke about me helping to fix her 9 hairs before we would go out. She was a hoot! All 4 feet 9 inches of her.

Even when I worked as a hairdresser, Gram would still expect me to take her shopping on my day off. She didn't seem to consider that I had worked all week. I would be as tired as a one-armed paper hanger, but I'd wake up and look across the street where Gram lived with Mom and Dad, and she'd be sitting on the front porch, all dolled up, with her handbag on her lap, just waiting for me to come pick her up to go shopping.

Grandma Maudie and I were very close when I was little. After Grandpa died, she and I shared a bedroom. Our house was very small and our bedroom closet was even smaller. So with Gram's love for clothes, her many dresses would be hanging on the backside of our closet door and the inside of the door to our bedroom as well.

Something I just remembered about our bedroom too is that there was a purple poster on my wall, with the text of The Lord's Prayer in silver glitter. There was a little girl on the bottom, kneeling in prayer mode. It actually scared me more than it comforted me. Something about the line "if I die before I wake" made the little girl in me wonder if I would awaken the next day myself.

I remember going to church with Mom when I was little too. There was always Sunday School for the kids, and the best part of the whole experience to me was the cookies and Kool-Aid that we were served afterward. Those cookies and Kool-Aid tasted better than any confection that I have ever tasted since. I guess I enjoyed the cookies more than the message. LOL

I truly do treasure so many of my childhood memories. I remember how delicious a big juicy piece of bubble gum tasted while drinking one of those Coca Cola's in an 8 oz. glass bottle. Or how peanuts poured into a Coke were oh so delicious and yummy. I was pretty sure that that's what Heaven must serve every day as a treat.

And try as I may, I have never been able to reproduce those tastes since. Must be something about the gazillion taste buds that you still have as a kid.

Back to Gram. The most 'cursing' Grandma Maudie would ever say was, "I'll be a dirty name". Too cute, right? She had a lot of cute sayings in her little Irish brogue that still make me smile when I think of them. I also remember that she would do a little Irish jig whenever the spirit moved her. I sure would like to be able to sit down with her and have a 'wee spot of tea' again and discuss all that has happened since she transitioned. I know she would have some sage advice for me. But one day, maybe she will share her feelings with me again. I can almost hear her saying, "Ya' just never know now, do ya?"!

Some of her memorable sayings were: 'Now isn't that grand?' Or, 'Top of the mornin' to ya now'. Or, 'You look like a shanty man in that get-up'. And, 'I'm so happy I could do a wee jig', and, 'I'll be a monkey's Uncle'.

Something reminded me of Grandma Maudie just recently when we were visiting with my stepson's family. His little 2-year-old son Gino had some food he was eating, backwash into his drink. My grandma called those food particles trolly-wags. I still remember my Grandma always telling me not to get any trolly-wags in her drink whenever I took a sip of her tea. I sure do miss that wee slip of a lady, wearing that housedress and a kitchen apron that covered her rounded belly.

My Mom, in comparison, could curse like a sailor – and often did, much to my embarrassment at times. But it never seemed to bother anyone else, even back then, when the times seemed to expect a more gentile attitude from women. But everyone loved my Mom just as she was. She was also generous to a fault on the one hand, and very frugal about other things on the other hand.

I still find myself using some of the expressions Mom used to say. I think she may have made them up but they stuck with me. Even my daughter Tracey uses some of them. And it makes me smile when she does. Like Jerkimer. That's what she called someone that she considered an idiot. And for something that she considered huge or a lot of, she used 'fifty-leven'. Do-ma-flatchy, what's it, and thing-a-ma-jig were for anything she didn't remember the name of at the time.

Mom was a women's libber way before it was fashionable. She was a very accomplished woman in business too, and she was the boss in our house as well. Dad never seemed to mind though. He was very low-keyed and had a passive, easy-going personality. Easy does it must have been Dad's subconscious life motto. It obviously worked because I rarely ever saw him angry.

I do remember one time though that he got really pissed. Mom could go on and on at times, but this one time Dad must have had enough. He had cleaned some fish in the kitchen sink and some fish blood had gotten on the kitchen rug. Mom was very angry and brought the rug to Dad where he was sitting in his chair. Mom stuck the rug right under his nose and was yelling at him about the blood on it. I remember holding my breath in anticipation of what would happen next. Well, I'll tell you what happened.

There was this one phrase that Dad used that would make Mom know she had gone too far. It was, "For Jesus Christ sake!" When Dad said that, Mom knew to be quiet. And he said that phrase that day, and I just sat there, frozen, afraid to let out the breath I was holding in.

Sure enough, Mom just walked back in the kitchen, with the bloody rug in hand, cleaned up the mess and kept her mouth shut. I breathed a sigh of relief. Mom didn't back down very often, but I have to admit that I sort of liked it when Dad used his 'special words' that could make Mom clam up! And there weren't very many occasions or people who could do that.

Mom was the President of my school's PTA. And she continued to be President even a year after I graduated. She also belonged to the women's charitable organization Beta Sigma Phi and was their National Convention Chairwoman one year. She was also a member of The Pilot Club of Hollywood, which was also a women's business club that did charity work in the city as well. Mom was also a council member of our local city government in Hollywood, Florida. Mom was an accomplished woman for sure.

Mom could be as tough as nails on the one hand and mush with me on the other…..after I married that is. And always with her grandkids. I will always have much admiration and respect for my mother and all that she accomplished, and how generous she was. I will never be the woman that she was, but I also know that she thought that I hung the moon and would kill anyone who would try to harm me. I miss you Mom. And I miss you too Dad.

I was blessed to have them both as my parents in many, many ways, and I will always be grateful to them and for my upbringing. Mom was very strict for sure. There were no Gold Stars handed out to me for just showing up. Getting good grades was mandatory. And Mom's word was law. But I'm proof positive that Mom being strict with me didn't harm my self-esteem. And I was raised was to be polite, have manners, and to be respectful.

I know that my parent's love and adoration for me, and the 'stick to it approach' to life they taught me, helped me get through many hard times and painful life experiences over the years. I must have gotten some of their good characteristics and qualities somewhere along the way because I made it through some pretty sad and hard times.

I also remember that my Mom had a very rough time with menopause. Mom was 31 when she had me, so when I was around 10 years old, she had full-blown, and early onset menopause. Mom called it 'the change of life'. She would have terrible spells of uncontrollable hypertension and feelings of claustrophobia. As a little girl, I worried that she would die before I grew up.

Hearing stories about my Grandma Maudie losing her own mother at such a young age, made me think that it was quite possible that my parents could die while I was young too. As I look back on how I was feeling at that time, it sounds selfish that I was thinking how my parent's death would affect me, and not so much about how it would affect them. I suppose as children we do have a narrow, if not selfish, perspective on life. But I guess it was a natural fear at that age for me.

A fun fact about Grandma Maudie and my Dad is that they were only 3 years apart in age. Dad was born in 1896 and Grandma Maudie was born in 1893. Dad was 22 years older than my Mom. But I never thought of him as being old enough to be a Grandpa while I was growing up.

Dad was always in good shape and he wore his black hair slicked back, and he had a great tan from working outdoors. He never did have many wrinkles to speak of. I can thank him for the good skin that I was blessed with. I suspect that he was a bit vain too because he used to use Men's Grecian Formula when his hair started to gray. And he always tilted his head a certain way when we took his picture as if he wanted to produce his best side in the snapshot.

Dad was a good looking man for sure! People used to say he looked like the old-timey actor Warner Baxter. And people said my Mom looked like the ole-timey actress Mary Astor. And I agree that they both did look like those stars.

Evidence of Dad's vanity was made perfectly clear when he got a little cancer on his lip. Probably from smoking those little Italian stogie cigars for years. He had the lip taken care of, and then he quit those stinky stogies for good! I can't say I was sorry about him quitting those smelly cigars.

I can still picture Grandma Maudie and my Dad having a wee cup of tea while watching Liberace playing piano on TV in the afternoons. And my Dad would play along sometimes on his accordion. These are some of my favorite memories of them. And I remember lying on the couch in the last weeks of my pregnancy with little Terry, and watching TV with them and enjoying some of that tea as well!

Grandma Maudie and Grandpa Bick had moved to Detroit where Grandpa worked as an undertaker. Grandpa liked to drink quite a bit. He was Irish after all. Some days he wouldn't come home and Grandma would walk up to the bar where she knew he would be and take the steering wheel off of his car.

Apparently, in the early 1900's, the steering wheels were removable so the driver could carry it away with them and prevent the unauthorized use of the vehicle. Sort of the original version of today's anti-theft devices. She did it partly to make sure he didn't drive while drunk, but I suspect that a larger part was to get even with him for not coming home.

I had heard many stories of how during prohibition, Grandpa would take an empty casket over to Canada and bring it back full of whiskey. I guess that is how he made a little extra cash for the family.

Back then he used a horse and buggy with an open flatbed on the back to haul the caskets. No one at the Canadian border ever thought, or wanted to take a peek inside the casket. Partially out of respect for the dead, but I'm guessing more so because they were spooked and didn't want to see a dead body. It was a good thing that they never did, or Grandpa would have been in a whole bunch of trouble!

Grandpa was known to wander off at times too. Mom told me when I was old enough to understand, that Grandpa had [delusion of grandeur]. That is a mental health condition that is associated with bipolar disorder and/or schizophrenia. He would say that he was the Mayor of the town or some other dignitary some days, and he would make up stories about how he held important positions at other times. We would just go along with whatever he was calling himself on any given day. But I do always remember Gramps smiling. Mostly toothless because he hated to wear his dentures. But surprisingly, he could eat an apple without teeth with no problem, and he could eat a corn cob clean!

Sometimes he'd be gone for days and even months. This left Grandma, who didn't drive, to be left at home alone with 3 children to tend to.

So Grandma found a job at a pie factory close by and worked many hours, standing on her feet all day to make ends meet. She had to find a way to support the family during Grandpa's sporadic little 'vacays'. She told me that some days she would drop a pie, on 'accident', just so she could bring it home as a treat for the kids. Grandpa would eventually make it back home and I can only imagine the ear thumping he would get. But they stayed together all of their many, many years because that's just what you did back in those days. Divorce was not an option. And everyone could feel that they loved each other. In sickness and in health, right?

Grandpa Bick had a drinking buddy that he always hung around with. Water always seeks its own level don't ya' know? They would get drunk and get into some pretty funny predicaments. One time my Grandma told me that she had just put up some new wallpaper in the breakfast room of their house, and Grandpa and his drinking buddy came home drunk, with a duck under Grandpa's arm. Grandma was mad as usual and asked where they had been. Grandpa took the duck from under his arm and started swinging it around while explaining how he got the duck. Well, poop spewed from the dead duck, all over the new wallpaper that Grandma had just put up. Ewwwwww.

Another time Grandpa and his buddy built a chicken coop in the back yard. The only problem was that they built the coop around themselves and couldn't get out. It seems as if those two were always running foul (or fowl in this case). And the story further explained that they had been having a few drinks as they were building the coop. No doubt!

There were always a lot of laughs in the house though. And I'm sure that's what kept them going through the lean times of The Depression. They had to use ration tickets for all the food and gas that they used. They told of a Victory Garden they had in the back yard so they would at least have vegetables to eat that didn't require them to use up their ration allotments on those items.

People still did die during the Depression, but many times the families didn't have the money to bury their loved ones. So Grandpa would get paid with bread if it was a baker's family member, or meat if it was a butcher's family member, or produce if they were in that kind of business. Heck, he probably even got paid with a DUCK one time. Hmmmmmmmm

Back in the day, funeral homes were in the undertaker's house. The family would live upstairs and the viewing rooms were downstairs, and the embalming and holding areas were in the basement. My mom told me about a time that she went downstairs for something in the basement and she heard a groan and saw a body move.

It scared the bejeezus out of her and she ran back upstairs to tell Grandpa that there was a live person in the basement. Most kids would have been frightened by dead people in their home, but having a person seem to be alive in the morgue portion of the house was more of an anomaly for mom. It turned out that the person had a bit of a hump on his back, and apparently when we die, we still have gases that can be expelled. This is what had happened to the corpse. He just expelled some gas and rolled over from his hump. Spookyyyyyy.

My Mom would help her Dad with the bodies in the morgue when she was just a young girl. Mom had actually wanted to be an undertaker herself at one time. But family responsibilities made it impossible for her to go to college, so she never did become a funeral director. She would tell me how she would often help with the dressing of the corpses. She would even have me face her and lean over so she could tie the bow on the back of my dresses when I was little. I thought it was odd, but then she told me that that's how she dressed and tied bows on the clothes of the bodies. That made it seem even creepier to me. Cue the Twilight Zone Music!!!!!

♪♪ Do-do-do-do / Do-do-do-do ♪♪

I would spend all of my summers in Detroit with Grandma and Grandpa Bickley. I never did meet my Dad's parents because they never left Italy. And I never had the chance to go over there while they were still alive. Or since actually. Ireland and Italy are definitely on my Bucket List. And I'd better get busy checking them off my list at my age – before I kick the bucket!

There were 12 children in my Dad's family. I can't even imagine the hard life Grandma Angela must have lived. There was no running water or electricity and she had to wash clothes down by the creek and haul drinking and cooking water back up to their house for her family. She cooked over an open fire in the fireplace and went to church whenever she got a chance. Which was mostly every day is what Dad told me. But she lived to be in her 90's, so I guess the saying that hard work never kills you is correct.

Just a side note: I've already told you my maternal grandmother's name was Maude and I just mentioned my Dad's mother's name was Angela. Since my mother didn't want to have any more children, she gave me both grandmother's names as my middle name. I could have actually become a nun with a name like mine - Shirley Angela Maude Recchia Pribisco Brady. Wellllll, a nun without the vow of chastity of course. *wink-wink*

CHAPTER 6

Summers in Detroit

When I was 5 years old, my Mom had had enough of this staying at home stuff and got a job as a bookkeeper. She loved me very much but she just wasn't cut out to be a stay-at-home Mom. She chose that job because she was very good with numbers; another gene that was not shared with me. Wow, my Dad didn't share his artistic gene with me and my Mom didn't share her gift of numbers with me. But someone in my past must have had the love of writing because I can sure yak it up on a keyboard. And I do love to write. It all balances out I guess and that's what makes the world go around.

I remember Mom dropping me off at pre-school and I'd sit on the stoop until the teacher got there. I suppose it was only for a few minutes before the teacher was expected to arrive, because my Mom was very cautious and sometimes even overprotective, much like the helicopter moms you see sometimes today. So I know she thought I was safe until the teacher did get there. Back in those days, you didn't have to worry as much about psychos taking children and doing heaven-knows-what with them like you do today.

Mom wouldn't even buy me a bike because she thought I'd get hurt. So I had to save my allowance and buy my own Schwinn bike when I was about 10 years old! I can still remember riding like the wind on that pretty blue bike!

I wasn't supposed to go swimming while I was spending the summers in Detroit either. But Grandma just didn't tell Mom, and swore me to secrecy. And we had some very nice times swimming in the Lakes during the summer – even though they were always freezing cold to this Florida girl!

Those summers I spent in Detroit are some of the most favorite memories I have of my childhood. My Mom's brother Uncle Bill and their sister Aunt Maggie lived in Detroit too. As did my Dad's brother Uncle Pete and his wife Aunt Susie.

Those times spent with all of my cousins were some fun, fun, fun times for sure. Uncle Bill and Aunt Jackie had 7 children (4 boys and 3 girls). There was Billy, Jim, Kathy, Bob, Rich, Barbara, and Nancy.

Aunt Maggie and Uncle Gordon had 2 girls - Bev and Cheryl. Uncle Pete had a boy and a girl (Rosemary and Gene), but they were older than me, so I played with my second cousin Gloria, who was the daughter of my cousin Gene. Uncle Pete's daughter Rosemary never had any children but the times I spent at her house conjure up many happy times for me too. And her cooking was also amazing. Cousin Rosemary just died recently. It's sad that so many of my cousins have passed.

Ro was the sweetest person and she would always take Mom and me out when Mom would come up for her 2-week vacation, just before my school year was about to begin again. It was always a treat when we would go downtown to the giant Hudson's Department Store to shop and have lunch.

The J.L. Hudson Building (Hudson's) was a 29 story department store located at 1206 Woodward Avenue, in downtown Detroit. Each floor had specific merchandise particular to that floor like you can see in the old-timey movies.

I remember one winter visit before Tiffany was born, we took Terry and Tracey to downtown Detroit and we went into Hudson's to visit Santa Claus. One entire floor of the store was full of Christmas joy. Choo-Choo trains carried wistful children along the tracks with dolls, and toy trucks, and every imaginable plaything that could be displayed on the shelves to ooh and aah over. And of course, the best part was sitting on Santa's lap and telling him what you wanted him to bring you for Christmas morning.

While we were in the store shopping and having lunch, it had snowed and we didn't realize it. When we came out of the store, my son Terry who was only about 2 ½ at the time started crying. When we asked him what was wrong, he told us that we would never be able to find our car with all the snow covering all the cars in the huge parking lot. Too cute!

I also remember that Hudson's had elevator operators. They would open the accordion grate-type doors and you could see through them what each floor offered for sale. The elevator operator would announce; "Second floor – women's apparel" or "Third floor – men's furnishings" or "Fourteenth floor – lingerie"....etc. The elevator operators always wore white gloves and a little black, flat-topped hat, and they were very professional and quite polite and helpful.

I can remember going to the iconic F.W. Woolworth and S.S. Kresge's 5 and 10 Cent stores as a kid too. They offered lots and lots of stuff that you could buy for a nickel or a dime. For Real! They were the frontrunners to the Walmart's and Dollar Stores of today.

Eating at the luncheonette counter was always a treat at the 5 and 10 cent store too. The clanging of the dishes as they were bussed and put into bins to be washed, and the hustle bustle of the shoppers – all 'dressed to the nines' I might add - were familiar and endearing sights and sounds back then. It was just a classier time to have lived in my opinion. No one would ever think of going shopping, or out to dinner, or go to the movies, or fly on an airplane, or go to church, without being fully, properly, and respectfully dressed. Whatever happened to that much more civilized way of living? Big Sigh......

Mom always made a shopping trip to Master's Candy on Grand River Avenue when she was in Detroit too. They had the best chocolate and hot fudge sauce. I remember boxes and boxes of candy and jars of hot fudge sauce that Mom would buy to bring back as gifts to our friends in Florida. My favorite was the chocolate haystacks. They were made of coconut, mixed into the milk chocolate and piled into haystack-looking lumps.

But I digress. Back to Grandma Maudie and Grandpa Bickley. They never liked to fly, so we would take the train up to Detroit each year when my school year let out. And I would fly back home with Mom when summer was over.

Those train rides were the most fun E-VAH! I still love trains to this day. There's a wistful feeling of nostalgia that surrounds thoughts of traveling by train. It was a much slower, more enjoyable mode of travel, I think. These days everyone is in such a hurry that they never take the time to notice the beautiful vistas that are passing by right under their own noses!

There would always be other kids on the train that were traveling to somewhere too, and we would play games and get to know each other over the few days it took to get from Hollywood, Florida to Detroit, Michigan.

I can still picture a time that I played a game of Tiddlywinks with a little boy on one trip when I about 8 years old. I also remember eating in the dining car sometimes, but not always, because it was a lot fancier and more costly than the food that the porters would bring on in baskets at the different station stops. The baskets of treats that were brought onto the train at the different stops would contain sandwiches and fruit and other snacks to purchase. WOW, the things I can remember from waaaay back when, and I can't remember what I ate for dinner last night! Oy Vey!

Sadly, there weren't any black people riding the train back then as I recall, except for the porters. I didn't think too much about it at the time. I can also recall that there were drinking fountains and bathrooms in public places in the South that were designated for whites only and separate ones for blacks. I have since come to realize, and be embarrassed by, what a very sad and very wrong part of our history that I was oblivious to at that age.

I don't remember my parents being or ever saying anything racist when I was a child. But these things that were happening weren't being pointed out to me how offensive it must have felt to the black people either. Proving that silence can do just as much harm as the deed in advancing transgressions. And I didn't realize that black people back then were only 'going along' with it out of fear for what would happen if they 'stepped out of line'. I am ashamed of being part of the white culture back then; a culture that could be so insensitive to other fellow human beings' feelings.

Not until the Civil Rights movement did many of us whites even think about what an awful practice it was to humiliate a whole race of people. It is still amazing to me, but it proves how we can mindlessly go along with the status quo, even when it's an absolute atrocity. Let me state right here and now that I am sorry for that whole part of our history. I know that isn't nearly enough. But, I personally am truly very sorry.

And I'm not so sure that the times or attitudes have changed all that much with some people who are still so prejudiced. And if they haven't changed by now, they probably won't ever be able to change. We can only hope that each generation will realize how horrible racism is and in that way, it may be a thing of the past someday. I sure hope so. But sadly, I don't see it happening in my lifetime. At least not as long as parents still keep teaching their children to hate.

My Grandma lived 6 blocks from Uncle Bill's house. My cousin Bev lived at Grandma's with her mom and dad and sister Cheryl. Grandma also had a boarder (renter) named Speedy, who lived in the butler's pantry. They didn't have a butler of course, but the room was big enough for a bed for Speedy, and he mostly ate his meals with the rest of the family. Bev and I would walk the 6 blocks almost every day to hang out at Uncle Bill and Aunt Jackie's house. You know, because they didn't already have enough kids hanging around their house. NOT…..

I remember the beautiful elm trees that lined each side of the streets. They were very tall and met in graceful arches at the tops, forming a gorgeous tunnel of leaves as you looked down the streets. They were also a perfect way to shade the homes back then since they had no air conditioning. In the 19th century, Detroit was known as the City of Trees. And they were truly magnificent. Sadly, years later the beautiful elm trees died from something called Dutch elm disease. The Detroit I remember is nothing like the Detroit of today. I'm sure glad that I got to enjoy her while she was still in all her glory!

I also remember a Dairy Queen that was right in the middle of the 6 block walk to Uncle Bill's house. Grandma would give us 25 cents each to get an ice cream cone every day. I still love Dairy Queen's soft-serve all these years later! Most likely because it's all wrapped up in the memories of those very special summers.

I would marvel at how Aunt Jackie kept everything going and everyone all cleaned and fed! My own small family consisted of just the 3 of us - so to see Aunt Jackie toast 3 loaves of bread at one breakfast sitting and peel a 10 pound bag of potatoes every night for supper, and she would send one of the kids up the street to the A & P for milk a few times a day because there wasn't enough room in the old-timey fridge for all the milk they would need for each day, totally amazed me! Can you imagine how much all of that would cost in today's market prices?

And all that laundry for all of the whole family! YIKES, just imagine all the lost socks in that household! At one time, Uncle Bill had bought Aunt Jackie a mangle for ironing clothes. It was this contraption that was supposed to make ironing easier for the 'lady of the house'. But with that many clothes to iron, the mangle seemed too complicated and ended up being used instead as a storage place for the piles of clean laundry. When anyone needed something ironed, they just hauled out the old handy ironing board and ironed what they were going to wear that day.

Speaking of a lot of laundry – there was a family of 23 kids that lived behind the alley from Aunt Jackie's house. You never saw the poor Mom – at least I never did. Probably because she was always in the basement doing laundry!!! I can't even wrap my mind around being pregnant for 23 years! They must have either been good Catholic's or very bad with the rhythm method used for birth control, or as it is also known, 'periodic abstinence'.

Something that I remember about Aunt Jackie is that she always had a clean and ironed 'house dress' on each day, and her hair was always just so. She used bobby pins to curl her hair at night so it would look nice and neat and curled in the morning. I will be forever grateful to her too for the way she applied her make up each day. I noticed that she always went over to the big window in the dining room because that is where the best light was to see that she had her make up on just right. I do that now myself because when you get older, you can't see with just the bathroom light. I have noticed many older women whose makeup looks downright scary, and I always think to myself that she didn't go to the window to put her makeup on. Thanks Aunt Jackie!

I remember each summer, as soon as I would get to my Grandma's house I would proceed to run up the stairs to the attic and all the way back down to the basement. And then back up again. There weren't many 2 story homes in Florida at the time, and no basements at all because Florida is at or below sea level, so basements weren't an option. So I loved, loved, loved the homes in Detroit, all with stairs galore! It's the contrasts in life that stand out most for us.

I even remember 2 houses down from Grandma's, there was a family named the Gardener's. They had a 2-story white house with a wrap-around porch and a white picket fence that was probably built in the early 1900's. I adored that house and I still love that style of architecture today.

I never went inside the Gardner house but I would have loved to. From my memory as a child, I remember Mr. Gardener as a tall, lanky man, that didn't smile very often, much like the pitchfork farmer in the painting 'American Gothic'. He didn't seem as if he were very fond of nosey kids lurking around his home either. So I always admired his lovely house from afar. I don't remember ever seeing a Mrs. Gardener or any children around the house now that I think of it. Maybe that was why he seemed so un-happy. Maybe he was just lonely.

My Grandma's house had 4 stories, if you count the attic and the base-ment, and it was made of red brick. There was a big front porch with an awning where you could sit and just watch what was going on in the neighborhood and enjoy the early evening air. There was also a small back porch that led to the backyard and the stand-alone garage. My cousins and I would play on that back porch and make believe it was our own little house. We had many good times in that back yard.

I remember cookouts and just sitting in chairs laughing and visiting with friends and family. I remember chasing lightning bugs and playing games with the other kids. I remember ears of corn roasting on the grill, alongside hamburgers and hot dogs. I remember tinfoil wrapped potatoes just thrown into the hot coals too. Even though they looked burnt on the outside, I remember them tasting oh so good, with a smoky sort of flavor to them.

Grandma and Aunt Maggie did the cooking at Grandma's house and we ate most of our meals in the basement because it was cooler down there. Michigan summers can get pretty hot and there was no air-conditioning back then. Just large window box fans that would blow outward on one side of the room and inward on the other side of the room, to take advantage of the cross ventilation when all of the other windows were open.

I can also remember many summers that I suffered from prickly heat rash. But being with all the family and cousins and aunts and uncles was well worth all the scratching. Thank goodness for baby powder.

Grandma and Grandpa had a pear tree in their front yard and I thought that was amazing. My Uncle Bill had a cherry tree in their backyard that also amazed me. I was only used to tropical fruits trees in Florida, so the fruit trees from up North were an oddity to me. And on the flip side, my Northern relatives were enamored with our citrus, avocados, mango trees and other tropical fruits, plants, and flowers that are so plentiful in Florida. I guess we all just take for granted what we have, and marvel at other people's things.

I remember being stung by a bee on my backside one day while I bent over to pick up a ripe pear that had fallen to the ground. I can still feel the sting of that wicked bee.

My cousin Bev and I would watch Shock Theater on Saturday night TV. It featured old, classic, horror films like Dracula, Frankenstein, the Werewolf, the Mummy, etc. Well, at least we tried to watch anyway. But when the spooky voice would come on and tell us to dim the lights, close the shades.....and lock the doors – and then the scary organ music would get real loud......we would usually be too afraid to watch for very long and hightail it up to our bedroom and try to fall asleep. Emphasis on 'try'.

I remember many nights that I cried myself to sleep because I missed my Mom and Dad. It wasn't that I wasn't having fun; I was just a little girl who must have felt a little insecure sometimes without her mommy and daddy.

My cousin Jim was always curious about our alligators in Florida and he brought a baby one home to Detroit after a visit with us one year. I later heard that it had escaped. I always pictured that gator growing large and being a menace to the city, like the sci-fi movie that came out years later with that same theme. Rut Roh!

I remember huge picnics that my Dad's side of the family would have in the many Detroit county parks. By huge I mean 50 to 100 people. Sisters of Aunt Susie and all of their families would bring baskets and baskets of food for all to share and eat. They brought fried chicken, potato salad, salami, all sorts of luncheon meats, tossed salad, Italian breads and sweets, fruits, sodas, sausage and peppers.......just about anything you can think of. There was no take-out food with those great cooks! And Aunt Susie and her sisters could sure cook some delicious food.

There were lots of things to play at the parks too; like baseball, swinging on the swings and the merry-go-round thingy's, playing badminton, and a lot of other fun stuff. It was always a really good time. People don't picnic very much anymore. I think families were a lot closer back in those days. And more easily entertained too. We were happy with a transistor radio to dance to and to just look up at the sky and count the stars when they came out. When was the last time you went out at night just to look at the stars? Yeah, I thought so. Me neither. But it's really a beautiful and serene thing to do. When I do look up at the stars now, it puts everything in perspective for me.

I remember when we would go over to visit Aunt Susie and Uncle Pete, we'd pull up the driveway on the side of their house and you could smell the aroma of spaghetti sauce cooking as it wafted up through the open basement windows. And BOY was it ever good. Mama Mia!!!!

Aunt Susie was a little bit of a thing, not even 5 feet tall. I can remember her making homemade pasta with a long wooden dowel, on a table that the legs had been shortened for her to work at more comfortably. She cut the dough by hand and it was so precise that you'd have thought that it was store-bought. But there was no store-bought pasta in Aunt Susie's house. Maybe in later years, but not when I was little. Thank goodness!

I remember freshly made spaghetti and pasta being laid out to dry all over the place in her basement that she would layer with waxed paper and put in boxes to freeze for later meals. And there was always a small garden out in the backyard that had tomatoes, basil, peppers, zucchini squash, and other veggies that were ready and ripe when needed. I'm quite sure those fresh veggies and spice plants were some of the reason that the end results were so magnificent and delicioso!

Aunt Susie always made homemade gnocchi when my Mom came up to visit because it was Mom's favorite. Gnocchi is a mix of mashed potatoes and dough, made into little round knobs. You boil them, just until they rise to the top, then drain them and put the spaghetti sauce and grated cheese on top. YUMMO!

The cheese for the pasta was always freshly grated from a huge block of imported cheese that was wrapped in cheesecloth and kept in the refrigerator.

And there was always fresh loaves of Italian bread in the house. You could use the bread to either dip it in the sauce that was cooking on the stove or to make a sandwich of sausage, peppers, meatballs and other meats that had been cooked in the sauce. Or use it sop up any sauce on the plate after you ate her delectable pasta. Win-win-win-win!

I love those memories because they are so full of tradition. Like helping Aunt Susie. It brings me right back to her basement, with all the smells of her sauce cooking on the stove, just as if I were back there right now.

Aunt Susie's sisters were always cooking too, and although each sister made her sauce the same way, each sauce tasted a little different. But it was all scrumptious. Aunt Susie's sisters weren't my blood Aunts, but I always considered them my very own anyway. You could just feel the love oozing out of those ladies. And they showed their love in the foods they prepared for the family, and for anyone who entered their homes. I remember Uncle Pete always saying......Eat, Eat, Eaaaaat!

Aunt Susie's name in Italian is Assunta and her maiden name was Gatti. I can still remember her father, Grandpa Gatti, would give me and the other kids a silver dollar each time we saw him. I sure wish I had kept all those silver dollars. They would probably be worth a lot today! But those memories will always be with me. He was just the sweetest little man.

My Dad would come up to visit some years, and he and his brother Pete, and all of their friends would speak to each other in Italian. I wish Dad would have taught me how to speak his country's language, but he never did. Dad always said that Italian was the most beautiful language of all. But I guess everyone thinks their own country's language is the best.

All the men would be listening to a baseball game on the radio, down in the basement or on the back patio, while their every wish was tended to by the women. I would marvel at everyone all talking in their native tongue and laughing and laughing and laughing. They must have had some pretty awesome times that they were reminiscing about. I remember my Dad would laugh so hard that he had to wipe happy tears from his eyes every so often with his handkerchief. Now that's a lot of happy memories!

Even though I have always been fiercely proud of my heritage, I remember thinking back then that I wouldn't want to marry an Italian man when I grew up, because it seemed to me that the men were kings in the marriage, and the women were just supposed to make sure the kings were taken care of. It's funny what you perceive when you are a child. But I don't think that I was very far off the mark when it came to the family hierarchy I observed back in those days.

Although there was deep love in the homes, I couldn't help notice how the whole family dynamic seemed to be heavily slanted in favor of the men. But I know that was in part because the men were the wage earners and most times the women stayed home to take care of the children and the house. And every whim that the man of the house might need! This was before we women realized our worth was just as valuable as the men's.

There was always a lot of laughter in my childhood years. My Grandpa Bick was also a very funny guy who was always telling jokes and off-colored limericks. My Uncle Bill was hilarious too. And there were always jokes and laughter going on in my Grandma Maudie's house. My son Terry was also a very funny guy! Terry and I had many a good laugh together, many times over, and I am so grateful for those memories.

Laughter is just so yummy! And just maybe, laughter played a part in how I was able to survive so many of the sorrows that I would have to face later on in life.

When my Mom would come up to Detroit for her 2-week vacation, she would take all of us kids to Edgewater Park. Edgewater Park was an amusement park and we all had a great time together riding the rides and eating the carnival-type food.

It was a very special treat for my cousins from Uncle Bill and Aunt Jackie because, with 7 kids, it was way too expensive for them to take everyone to the amusement park very often. But Aunt Katie (that's what they called my Mom) would haul all of us down to the park and she paid for everything! Good times for sure! This is a great example of how generous Mom was.

I remember looking forward to going to the Michigan State Fair each year too. It was like Edgewater Park on steroids. Mom would haul a bunch of us kids to the State Fair and we'd see all the exhibits and ride the rides, and look at all of the animals waiting to win a ribbon. And we would eat all the junk......errrr....carnival-type food imaginable.

I can still taste the corn on the cob that was roasted to a golden glaze on metal grates, over open flames that everyone just HAD to have. And huge turkey legs that were eaten as they were carried around the fairgrounds, making the people looked as if they were from some Old English Kingdom of long ago.

The fair was spread out on acres and acres and it was just a magical event to experience each year. Especially for my cousins and me. And Mom of course. In fact, I think Mom may have enjoyed it more than we kids did. My Mom never saw a carnival she didn't love.

Thinking about the State Fair and all the animals that were judged there reminds me of how Terry and Tracey were members of FFA (Future Farmers of America) in their little country school in Alva, Florida. I've told you how funny my Terry was, and sometimes he didn't even know he was being funny. Well, Terry had brought home his Membership Card for FFA and told me how they had had to give him another one because he messed up the first one. When I asked why, he told me that in the space where you fill in your personal information, that in the space marked Sex___, he had written in "not yet". That was my Terry. Always a hoot and always keeping us laughing.

Mom had always made a good living, and with Dad's income added to their finances, we never lacked for anything. We weren't wealthy by any means, but they did okay for those days. I can remember seeing some pretty big checks from Dad's cement jobs that just sat on our mantle for a time before Mom took them to the bank. Mom had a head for figures and she always saved their money. They had a pretty sweet 'cushion' in their later years, and they were what you could call 'comfortable'. I feel that Mom's generosity is why we never wanted for anything in life. Life gives back to us what we offer to life.

Mom would always do something big for her 'little' brother Bill each year when she visited him in Detroit. One year it would be new carpet for the house, another year it would be some furniture or an appliance they may have needed. Stuff like that. And whatever she did for Uncle Bill, she would give the same amount of money to her 'little' sister, Aunt Maggie. Aunt Maggie and Uncle Gordon lived in Grandma Maudie's big house with her, so she didn't need the carpet or furniture. But I'm sure they always appreciated the cash.

I remember my cousin Nancy, who was Uncle Bill and Aunt Jackie's youngest child, told me years later how she 'hated' me when she was little because when I would come up for the summer, I always had nice, new clothes and seemed to have everything a little girl could ever want.

Sadly, my cousin Nancy has passed now, but she and I kept up our 'cousin lovin' all through the years. She told me several times after we grew up that she did love me very much and we laughed at how her perspective must surely have been skewed by being the last of 7 children in the family.

I loved Nancy a whole lot too! Her experience surely must have been one of hand-me-downs, so seeing me come up each summer with all new clothes must have irked her as a child. I don't have memories of her clothes being any different than mine. But I guess that came from my own experience of growing up without having to share or compare.

My memory of Nancy as a little girl was that she was very pretty and she had the most beautiful blonde hair that she would always 'allow' me to brush. It must have been the future hairdresser in me that liked to play with her hair.

Nancy and I 'spoke' through IM on Facebook a lot during the last part of her illness because she had lost her ability to speak. Nancy fought hard, but sadly she lost her battle to Lou Gehrig's disease (ALS). We didn't have the chance to visit each other often, but I fondly remember a visit she had with us in Florida, and we really did have a blast! Thanks to Facebook, I can still keep in touch with Nancy's daughters Lisa and Becky, and their families – and my other family members that live a distance away too.

On Nancy's visit, my daughter Tracey, Nancy and I went down to Bayside in Miami and rode the horse-drawn carriage all around and we ate, and shopped, and laughed. And laughed some more. I am so grateful now that we had that visit. Nancy had the most infectious laugh and she was always smiling that big beaming smile that I will always miss about her. Nancy always called me Shirl. I sure wish I could visit with her one more time and have her call me Shirl again!

My Aunt Maggie worked in a grocery store across from Grandma's house on the corner of Greenfield and Plymouth Road in Detroit. Aunt Maggie and Grandma Maudie never learned to drive, so the grocery store was very convenient for Aunt Maggie to be able to walk to work. Can you ever imagine not driving? My cousin and I used to drive the family Buick all around the cemetery when we were only 10 or 11 years old. We used to visit the cemetery quite a lot back then. I still remember so many of these details, all these years later. Like Grandma's address was 11624 Winthrop Street and their phone number was Vermont 61160.

Back then the phone numbers had a name of a place as the prefix part of the number. There was only one phone in the house and it was black with a cradle that the listening and speaking part rested in. The phone sat on a shelf that was carved into the wall, right at the base of the stairs that led to the upstairs bedrooms and bathroom. It had a long spiral cord attached from the phone base to the cradle. It had a dial as opposed to the phones we have today that have a tone when you 'dial' the number. Funny how we still refer to it as dialing the phone. We had a party line, which meant there were 2 or more people who used the same line. There was a different ring for each household, so you knew when to answer – or when to just listen in. LOL, just kidding…….or am I?

Being from the Motor City, my cousin Bev and I would know every make and model of car that Detroit made. I know my uncles didn't make a ton of money, but somehow they always managed to drive big, new, shiny cars. I remember my Uncle Bill driving to Florida one year with all 7 kids in their big Buick Le Sabre Sedan. Including him and Aunt Jackie, that was 9 people all packed in the car like sardines in a can – for a 1500 mile ride. I can't even imagine all the potty stops for that trip! Never mind 7 kids yelling 'are we there yet?'

In Detroit, all of us kids would hang out at the park during the day, or at Uncle Bill's house. The girls would fix each other's hair or sing songs along with the radio and the guys would just be trying to look cool, with their hair slicked back like the dudes in the movie Grease.

You didn't really have to worry much about getting kidnapped back in those days. It was perfectly safe to be out all day, just as long as you were home by suppertime. There were no cell phones and we didn't wear watches, but you just knew when it was time to head back home. I guess we had an internal time sensor in us back then – or we just got hungry. And the street lights coming on helped too. Ha!

Sitting in the Elias Big Boy's Drive-In parking lot was also the big thing back then, once the guys got cars. All the guys with their souped-up cars would drive in and out of the parking lot all night, showing off their pride and joy cars. And they would rev their engines when they passed by a pretty girl. It was just like the TV show Happy Days. And we girls would make our hair pouf up about a foot off of our heads and wear tons of makeup so the guys would be enamored by us. I wish I had owned shares in Aqua Net hairspray back then!

I remember my cousin Kathy used to apply her make-up and do her hair at night before she went to bed. Kathy wasn't a 'morning person' and she didn't want to have to do it in the morning.

We wore Bobby Socks and Saddle Oxford shoes, and crinoline slips under our skirts to make them stand out a mile. Oh, and virgin pins. They were these circular gold toned pins that you wore on the Peter Pan collars of your blouse, to show that you were still a virgin. Imagine that. Back in the day, you were respected if you stayed a virgin until you married. Today, you're thought to be weird if you stay a virgin much beyond the 6th grade. Kinda sad, don't ya think? I guess that is just one sign of how generations don't understand how the other thinks. And why the joke about getting old is so funny and true – "Why do people die when they get old? THEY WANT TO!"

Several other of my cousins have passed now, as have my Aunts and Uncles and Grandparents, and Mom and Dad. Sometimes I just think about how one day we are here…..and the next day we aren't. But life does go on. I am just grateful that I have so many wonderful memories. If I could give anyone one piece of advice about having a life that will be satisfying long after those good old days pass us by, it would be to make as many special memories as you can, because they will surely give you a lot of comfort in your golden years.

I can honestly say that I can close my eyes and have the most glowing, magical feelings while remembering the times that I have had throughout my lifetime. It makes me feel so blessed.

Mom always made sure she planned a visit to see Mrs. each year. And no, I didn't leave her last name out – that's just what everyone called her. Mrs. was an old friend of my Grandma Maudie's. Grandma told me that 'Mrs.' had a huge tragedy in her life when she was younger. Her entire family was lost in a fire. I think it was in Nova Scotia if I remember correctly. She had to start a new life and ended up in the little town of Sandwich, just over the Detroit River in Canada. She eventually married again and had more children. The man she married was my grandpa Bickley's best buddy.

She was a widow again by the time I was able to meet her. Her home didn't have indoor plumbing, so we had to use the outhouse if we needed to 'go'. I remember that I didn't especially enjoy the idea of using her outhouse facilities at all. It was much too stinky in there for me!

Some of the good food memories about visiting Canada and Mrs. included the fish n' chips that we would always have. They served the French Fries (called chips), in paper cones and the fish was served was on newspapers. And you always put malt vinegar on both. I still love vinegar on my fish n' chips to this day.

Another food-related memory is of my Mom buying Canadian bacon and Colby Cheese during our visits to Canada. Mom always swore that the Colby Cheese in Canada was the best in the world. You weren't supposed to bring any foodstuff back across the border, but Mom always seemed to smuggle it in somehow. That smuggling gene must have been handed down to her from Grandpa. Ha!

CHAPTER 7

Life in 'Old Florida'

Back in Florida, I just played outside all day as a child, and mostly on barefoot. I still remember the sand spurs that I'd sometimes get in my feet. But actually, being barefoot so much of the time makes your feet pretty tough, so the occasional sand spur was a rarity. Mom always kept the iodine and mercurochrome handy for those times that I did get a sand spur though. And we'd keep watch that there was no red line going upward toward the heart from the sore spot, because that was a sign that you could get lockjaw from tetanus.

I noticed a lot of the other kids had impetigo back then too. "Impetigo is a common and highly contagious skin infection that mainly affects infants and children".

You could always tell who had impetigo by the purple gentian violet lotion that was used as a topical remedy. The purple spotted skin was a sure giveaway. This was before the topical antibiotic creams that are so readily available these days in drug stores. I never did get impetigo though. I assume Mom kept a pretty good eye out for that sort of stuff.

I do remember Mom lamenting how she took extra special care of me, but somehow I would still come down with a cold or something – and how the other kids in the trailer park were just left to their own devices and waded in puddles and such, and never seemed to get the sore throat or ear aches that I would occasionally get. Mom would say that God takes care of children and drunks. I didn't know what she meant back then though.

Mom would use Musterole (a rub like Vicks, but much stronger and more potent) when I would come down with a cold. She would rub the Musterole all over my chest and neck. It had such a strong, pungent odor that it felt as if it could take your breath away, instead of helping you breathe better!

Back in the day, women used pads when they had their menstrual periods. The pads were long and had extra material on each end that attached to an elastic belt with a metal cinch on each end. Mom used to put one of her pads around my neck and pin it in the back with a safety pin, to keep my neck warm and supposedly make me better faster. But I looked pretty weird if you ask me.

Mom always warned that you had to make sure you bathed and got all of the Musterole off the next morning. I never did ask what would happen if you didn't, I just knew it was the law of the land in our house.

I remember our neighbors, the Fritchey's, lived one street over from us in Hollywood. They were tomato farmers. We kids would play on their low-rise, one-axel flatbed and if you stood on one end, it would drop down and you could run up to the top and it would drop back down again on the other side. Much like a giant see-saw. These were the sorts of things we did as kids. We would also draw circles in the dirt and play marbles, and play jacks and hopscotch on any hard surface we could find. And of course, there was always the game of Tag and Rover, Red Rover. No electronic devices for us. But we always had lots of fun! And we kept quite slim from all the running around we did. A treat back then would be an apple or an orange. Candy and cake were only for holidays or special occasions. So that helped to keep us thin and healthy too.

The Fritchey's had a bunch of kids. I played mostly with Wanda. She had a twin brother named Wayne. I loved to go over to the Fritchey's to play. Their house always had someone coming in our out of their slamming screened back door. I remember their Dad always seemed to be lying in his bed, right as you came into their house. He was a very heavy set man and I remember that he always called me what sounded like Chair-ly to me. He would say, "Heyyyy Chair-ly, how are you doing today?"

There were always tomatoes in their kitchen in some form or another. Ripe tomatoes on the kitchen table, alongside not quite ripe ones. And some that looked like they were rotting too. And always stewed tomatoes on the stove. And flies! Flies all over everything. There was no air-conditioning in their house, so the house flies and little fruit flies just loved to hover over the tomatoes.

My mom would scratch her head in amazement when I would ask if I could eat at the Fritchey's because she knew about the flies too. And although there was always something good to eat at our house, I chose a lot of the time to eat at the Fritchey's because I just wanted to be around other kids. And Mom said that I would rather eat hot dogs and beans at the Leicht's house with all their kids too, instead of whatever she was serving for us at home.

The Sandora's lived across the street from the Fritchey's. I remember the Dad, George, used to get so mad at the kids for putting their hands on the walls, that he painted all the walls in the house black! He also used to get mad when the boy children took all of his socks, and he didn't have any left when he needed to wear them. So, his remedy was that he only wore red socks. Bright red socks at that! And no one else had better be wearing red socks in the house or they'd have hell to pay!

George's wife Margaret didn't 'pay him no mind' – as she was known to say a lot of the time. The Leicht's were also our neighbors. They had met Mom and Dad when we first moved to Florida. Mom told me that the first place they parked their little Airstream type trailer was in Ojus, Florida. The story Mom heard was that it was named that when a man called home to tell his family that he had made it to Florida and when they asked where in Florida – he said, 'Oh…..Jus Florida'. I can't swear if that's a true story though.

For some reason, Mom and Dad pulled up their trailer stakes and moved to Hollywood, and into another trailer court. And that's where they met the Leicht's. Dot Leicht and my Mom were besties before the term BFF was even a thing. My Dad and John Leicht were buddies too and they used to go to the dog track and bet on the dog races. They didn't have enough money for both of them to pay to get in back then, so one would wait outside the fence and the other one would go in and place their bets. And they'd take turns the next time for who would go in and who would wait outside.

Mom and Dot didn't hit it off right away though. One of the reasons was because my Mom kept her wooden clothespins (used to hang the wash outside) in a cloth clothespin bag. Mom always brought it in with the clothes when she took the laundry off of the line. That way, her clothespins stayed all nice and new looking. If you left the pins on the line, they would discolor and put little black marks from the metal hinges on the clean laundry the next time you hung the laundry out to dry.

Well, Dot didn't take her clothespins off the line, so she was always short of pins. She would ask to borrow them from Mom, and after a few times that they didn't make it back to Mom, she asked Dot the next time she asked to borrow them if she was asking to HAVE them to keep or just borrow them? I remember Mom's saying was, "Neither a lender nor borrower be." I guess that went for clothespins too. And apparently, Mom's generosity didn't extend to clothespins.

They eventually did work it out with the 'borrowing' stuff, and if Dot or Mom borrowed from each other, they always made sure to 'pay it back'. Mom said it was the best way to stay friends and not have feelings fester because of something the other friend did or didn't do.

Mom was always an upfront kind of person. No one could ever say that they didn't know where they stood with my Mom. Not E-VAH! Mom always told me not to gossip too, because the same people who talk TO you about other people, will be the same people who talk ABOUT you to other people when you're not around. Mom always had great advice.

Mom always kept me dressed like a doll, in cute little dresses when I was little. Dot would always offer to iron my dresses for Mom, and of course Mom was happy to oblige her. Mom said that Dot just loved ironing little girls' clothes. So it was a win-win for both of them! I remember cold-starching was the method used back then. It's where you'd have to soak your item in a starch solution and then let it dry. And then you would sprinkle the garment with water and put the rolled up shirt or whatever you are going to iron in the refrigerator – or icebox back then!

That made it easier to get the wrinkles out of the cotton material. And we ladies think we have it bad when we use starch that you just spray on!

I still remember the iceman bringing big blocks of ice to the trailer court when I was little. He used these huge metal pick tongs to carry the ice. The iceboxes were small and made of wood, with a bin inside for the ice, to keep the food cool. The iceman would chip off pieces for us kids to eat as a treat. And it really was a treat on those hot Florida summer days. I guess that's where the term 'chip off the old block' came from!

The Leicht's and Mom and Dad bought adjoining property at some point in Hollywood. They put their trailers on their property first and built their houses later, once they had saved up enough money. And yes, they were trailers and not mobile homes. Trailers refer to having your 'home' trail behind your vehicle. And that's exactly how Mom and Dad brought our trailer down when they came to live in Florida.

When we weren't living in the trailer court any longer, with a communal bath area, Dad built a cement brick and stucco bathroom on our property. Then Dad eventually built our house around the existing bathroom! We were never a family to waste anything. One of my Mom's favorite sayings was, "Waste not - Want not."

Mom and Dad and the Leicht's were very, very good friends for many, many years - actually until John and Dot died. And the Leicht's even went with Terry and me for our 'run-away marriage elopement'. More on that later. And years later, my husband Terry would race Stock Cars for John at the Hollywood Speedway, which is long gone by now.

I can still remember living in that small trailer when I was still a toddler. It couldn't have been any bigger than 16' long by 8' wide. They were some tight quarters to be sure, but we spent a lot of our time outdoors back then. There was no A/C, so the outdoors was a way to get some fresh air and not swelter in the aluminum can.....errrrrr, trailer. We mainly used the trailer for sleeping and eating. Mom cooked our meals in the little, itty, bitty kitchen. I remember the men BBQ'd a lot too. Especially in the summertime when it was just too hot to cook in the trailer.

At night, Dad would listen to the radio and Mom would read. My crib was right next to the built-in double bed that Mom and Dad slept in. I can still picture me standing at the end of my crib, peering out at Dad and whimpering for him to come and get me, while he was listening to the radio. All with warnings from Mom not to dare.

Dad must have won a few of those battles because I remember sitting on his stomach while he laid on the couch and listened to the radio. The Lone Ranger or a baseball game, or some other comedy show would entertain us on that little radio. It was kept on a shelf above the couch. That was over 60-something years ago Peeps! Da-yum good memory, right?

Mom often told how scary it was when we all came down to Florida with that small trailer behind their old red Ford pick-up truck. There were not any interstate highways for the route they took back then. They came by way of Hwy 25E and she said going around the mountains almost scared her to death.

Mom loved to tell of a time that they stopped at one place on the way down for some breakfast. It was in the mountains and it was really, really REALLY rustic. She told a funny story about ordering home fried potatoes with her eggs. The woman, who Mom said looked like Ma Kettle, asked her what home fried potatoes were. 'Ma Kettle' actually called them taters. (Of course she did).

Mom explained that they were potatoes and onions that were cut up and cooked in a skillet until they were browned. The woman yelled to the back of the shack.....uhhhh......store and said, "Pa, git out here and listen to how this here Yankee Lady sez how to cook her taters." They did make them as Mom instructed, and were very good. I bet they had them on the 'menu' from then on. See, Yankees and Southerners can git along – iffin they're a mind to.

By the time I was 8 years old, I was expected to have dinner on the table when Mom and Dad got home from work. Nothing grand. Just a meat and a vegetable, and a salad. Remember that I told you that I would get back to the fact that Mom was adamant about not making me a spoiled brat? This was one example.

Yes, I did get way more 'things' than a lot of kids that had to share with their siblings, but I was expected to do my share around the house too. Light stuff when I was young, like helping with the housework and making light meals and keeping my room picked up – AT ALL TIMES! And when I was 16, Mom got me a bright shiny red Chevrolet Malibu. With the caveat that I pay for all of my gas, oil changes, and tires as needed.

I was expected to keep it washed and to keep the inside clean at all times too. And Mom made it clear that if I were ever to get a speeding ticket, she'd take the car back. And I knew that she meant it. Oh yeah.....I knew she meant it for sure!

Most every Saturday we'd go to the 163rd St Shopping Center in Miami. It was called a shopping center because it wasn't enclosed. The mammoth enclosed malls weren't a thing yet. Many times I would bring a friend along to go shopping with us. Whatever Mom bought for me on those times, she always got something for the friend as well.

But Mom was also a firm disciplinarian. If I ever did anything to get grounded and she gave me 6 weeks of being grounded – she didn't mean 5 weeks and 4 days. It was 6 weeks, PERIOD – end of story. It does tend to make you think twice about disobeying when you know your punishment will be enforced.

I didn't misbehave very often because if I did, there was Dad's razor strap that was always hanging in the bathroom to remind me what was in store if I didn't behave. Dad used a straight razor to shave and the razor strap was used to sharpen the blade. I will admit that she did use it on me a time or two. But as I said, I was usually a pretty well-behaved child. DUH!

Mom might have been put into jail for whipping me if we had lived in today's times. But I turned out pretty well, if I say so myself. So it didn't do any permanent damage to my self-esteem. That's not to say that my punishment wouldn't have affected another child differently. But this is my story.....not anyone else's. And I realize that corporal punishment may not be called for, but boundaries or any sort of punishment do seem to be lacking in today's culture. It doesn't seem as if children are given any consequences for their actions.

I have experienced many decades here on Earth School. That means that I have witnessed my grandparents, my mom and dad's, my own childhood, my children's, my grandchildren's and now my great grandchild's generations. So, I can fully attest that times and attitudes have changed.

Each generation feels differently about how to raise children, and about morals, manners, and just about every other aspect of life. And the pendulum does swing back and forth a lot about either being too soft or too hard on children, and on most aspects of life.

Many parents may look back on how we raised our own children and wish we had done some things differently. But as long as we acted out of love and concern for the child, I think children are pretty resilient.

When I was growing up there was none of this fixing one thing for supper for one family member and something different for another member of the family. There were 2 choices in our house – take it or leave it. And another thing about our meals was that Mom always said to take all you want, but eat all you take. I would be lectured about some starving child in China or Africa or some other far off place whenever I balked at eating all of my supper.

I know the Moms of today don't agree with that method of childrearing, but that's the way it was in my house growing up. And if my Mom were still around, I'd tell you to take it up with her – if you dared. Ha, Ha!

I attended Hollywood Hills Elementary School until the 4th grade and then the school district boundaries were changed. Then I went to Stirling Elementary School in Fort Lauderdale for 4th – 6th grade. Then onto Olsen Junior High in Dania for 7-8-9th grade, and then onto South Broward High in Hollywood again until I graduated 12th grade. That sounds like a lot of different towns, but they are all pretty closely connected.

Believe it or not, I'm still friends with a lot of the 'kids' I went to high school with. And just a few years ago we had our 50th high school reunion and many of the alumni came back to attend. There are a lot of classmates that never left the area too. Why would they? Living in Hollywood and Fort Lauderdale is like living in Paradise.

The reunion was organized by our very own Queen Susan Abrams Heyder. She is the awesome glue that keeps us all together. And the reunion was spectacular. I don't know many people who could say that they stay in touch like the SBHS Bulldogs, Class of 1966 do! I wasn't in the 'In Crowd' in high school, but that doesn't seem to matter the longer you are out of school.

Some classmates even meet for dinner every few months at local restaurants, just to visit with each other. And Queen Susan orchestrates those get-togethers as well. So, thank you Queen Susan! You ROCK! And I'm just happy to be a loyal subject in your realm.

I always made good grades in school. As if I had a choice!! My future husband Terry went to a private school that was close to SBHS. We would meet up most days and have lunch together off campus. We would go to Yum-Yum Castle for burgers and curly fries or across the street from SBHS to Scott's Drive-In for the juiciest burgers in town. I remember their signature burger was called the 'Alaskan'. It had a 'special sauce' on it that made it taste awesome. My mouth waters just thinking about it.

Terry and I were pretty much joined at the hip during high school, so we didn't hang out much with any of the other kids. We did go to the National Guard Armory in Fort Lauderdale for the dances and we would see the other kids there, but we mostly stayed to ourselves. Not that we were anti-social or anything. Terry worked as an apprentice cabinet maker after school, and we would go out for dates on the weekend. So that left little time for other socializing.

This brings me up to graduating high school and onto Cosmetology School. I finished my 1200 hours of cosmetology school in 1967 and got a job right away at Altaire's Salon in the Hollywood Mall. That's the same mall that Adam Walsh is remembered for, as being abducted from and murdered in 1981.

Terry and I married when we were each just 19 years old. We weren't of legal age in the State of Florida and his parents didn't want him to marry so young, so we 'ran away' to Valdosta, Ga. I put that in quotes because running away for us meant that my Grandma Maudie went along with us as a chaperone, and my Mom and Dad and their best friends the Leicht's came up after the 3-day waiting period that is Georgia law, to see us married.

I remember sitting in the judge's chambers and him asking us – with a very southern drawl - if we understood that there was a 3 day waiting period. What he was getting at was the inappropriateness of us staying together while we were unwed. Boy, how times have changed.

At first, we didn't know where he was going with this question, but when we figured it out, we told him that my Grandma was with us as a chaperone. He smiled and seemed quite relieved and told us that was, "Fine then, just fiiiine!" So after the 3 days of waiting and staying at the Howard Johnson's motel in Valdosta, Ga., my parents and their friends the Leicht's came up and Terry and I were married. Tah Dahhhhh!

Just like that, two kids were married....and then what? We said our goodbyes to my mom, dad, grandma and the Leicht's, and then we were on our own. I was a virgin when we got married, so I was terrified when I thought of what was expected of me on our first night together. We got a bucket of Kentucky Fried Chicken to take back to our motel room and then I cried and cried. Terry was so kind, sweet and gentle, and he didn't get upset with me at all. He just drove us right back home. With the car smelling of fried chicken all the way.

When we got there, Mom and Grandma were very surprised to see us. Dad was already in bed. We had almost beaten them back home. Grandma was shocked that I hadn't done my 'wifely duty' as she called it, and she scolded me and made us go right over to her trailer home that was on the next street over from my parent's home. How embarrassing!

We lived in Grandma's trailer home for a while until Mom and Dad built a new home across the street from their old home. And then we lived with them until Terry built us our own home – right across the street from Mom and Dad. Do you see a pattern here? Uh....yeah.

A few months after we married, we had a reception and both families came, along with many of our friends and extended family to celebrate our marriage. And all was finally right in our world.

Terry owned a plumbing company and also built homes when we married. He was young but he was very smart and very responsible. Terry had a very kind and well-respected construction mentor in Bob Chambers, who was an established builder in Hollywood. I think Bob built most of the homes back then in the upscale neighborhood known as Hollywood Hills.

Chambers took Terry under his wing and helped him a lot to get started in building homes and duplexes. And my Mom helped with the accounting of the business books for Terry.

Terry was getting permits and building loans from the bank when he wasn't even 21 yet. My Mom knew the heads of the banks in town, and it always helps 'who you know'.

When Terry did turn 21, the president of one of the banks almost had a seizure when he realized that Terry had not been liable for any of the loans that the bank had been granting him. But Terry always did pay his construction loans. Character and honesty was a coveted asset and something to be proud of back then, and Terry had both. What a concept, eh? Concepts that seem scarce these days.

Terry was a big hunter back then and he went out to the Everglades almost every weekend. Me? Not so much. He actually built a hunting camp out there in the boonies, off of Alligator Alley, in the swamp. The guys always ate what they shot, so it wasn't like they were killing just for fun.

They brought the building supplies out to make the camp piece by piece and used Terry's swamp buggy to take the pieces from the roadside to the camp. I don't remember how he got the permit to use the property in the Everglades, but he did. They even rigged up some electricity with a generator so they could see at night and have refrigeration while they were there for the weekend. There were bunk beds for the hunters to sleep in, and a kitchen, a sitting area, and a bathroom with all the comforts of home. Well, all the comforts of a hunting camp out in the boonies, way out in the Everglades type of home.

He was so proud of it and after it was finished, he brought me out to see it. Not having a mint placed on your pillow when you are staying at a motel is camping to me. But this was a whole other dimension to me. He wanted me to spend the night there, but I just couldn't. I guess I acted like a Prima Donna would. He had taken me out on his airboat before, and all I could see were the red eyes of hundreds of alligators laying on the bank, just waiting for their next meal. Presumably me. But I think the guys liked it better when it was just the guys who stayed there, without women.

One time that Terry took me out to the swampy boonies, the airboat started taking on water and I became ballistic and was screaming to get me out!!! Poor Terry was bailing out the water as fast as he could so he could get the airboat going and get me safely back to civilization. He didn't offer to take me out very often after that. And I didn't ask to go back either.

I continued to work at Altaire's until I was 8 and a half months pregnant with our firstborn. Terry was born on June 16th, 1970 at Hollywood Memorial Hospital.

Being a new mom was awesome. I loved dressing him up and taking him out. Sometimes we would visit my friends, former customers, and co-workers at the beauty shop.

Baby Terry didn't like to sleep very much and he was a very active baby. In addition to having tummy problems. He would projectile vomit and we worried that he wasn't keeping enough down to stay healthy. But thank goodness he was a healthy baby after all, and he grew up to be a tall 6'2" gorgeous hunk of a man.

I remember little Terry waking up every few hours and I'd feed him and snuggle with him and then put him back in the swing so he would fall back asleep for a bit. In fact, swinging in the swing was the only way that he would go back to sleep. And the only way anyone else in the house could get any sleep at night too.

Back in those days, the infant swings weren't battery operated, and we used his so much to get him settled, that I must have stripped the gears. In the middle of the night, you'd hear the grinding gears as I wound up the swing for it go back and forth to soothe him – and us. God bless Mom and Dad who loved us so very much that they didn't complain at all.

And my Mom surely did love our little Terry. I had always been #1 with Mom and now I was lagging way behind in 2nd place. Mom had always wanted a little granddaughter, so when I came out of the recovery room, after giving birth to Terry, I told her that I would be back soon to have a little girl for her. Little did I know how prophetic that was because 15 months later we had Tracey!

Mom did love all of her grandchildren very much. Someone even had a license plate made for the front of her car that said, "Let me tell you about my grandchildren'. But there was no mistaking that Terry was her favorite. After we had had all 3 children, the girls used to laugh and say that they insisted on going in 3 ways on any gifts for Mom, because unless it was from Terry, she seemed to act as if it were chopped liver! I'm just glad that the girls were able to laugh it off!

I also remember that I was such a newbie of a Mom that I would put Terry's baby seat right outside of the shower when I bathed so that I could keep an eye on him at all times. Think Helicopter Mom here again.

It's so funny to think back at how much peril our kids were really in when you remember the old-timey, over-the-seat car seat thingy's that we used back in the day. And how our kids always rode in the front seat, without seatbelts, even when they were little. It's a wonder they survived at all. I can still remember the 'mom arm-crossover' we used to use to keep the kids from falling forward when you had to brake fast. OY!

Big Terry continued to go to the Everglades camp on the weekends and I remember my friends used to say that they would never 'allow' their husbands to do that. I'm grateful that I was mature enough to realize that a young man with so many responsibilities needed an outlet, and I never gave him grief about his hunting. I also thought to myself, why would I want to stop someone I loved from doing what they loved? I see wives today that don't seem to consider that their husbands' need time for themselves, just as we wives do. That is a recipe for resentment in the making. I love the saying, "Selfishness is not doing as you please – it's expecting others to do as you please." BINGO!

The funny thing is that my own Mom was never a big lover of little kids. She was good to them and always very generous with her nieces and nephews.......but she could only take little ones in small doses. Pun Intended. But that all changed when we had our three children. You would have thought that they were the 2nd, 3rd, and 4th coming!!!!

Terry and Tracey were so close in age that they were almost like Irish Twins (babies born less than 12 months apart). At first, I was a little afraid of how I would manage 2 babies at once. It was more tricky than having twins because little Terry walked at 9 months of age, so I had to run around after him and still tend to our precious little Tracey. But Tracey was not as active as Terry was, and she was happy to sleep most of the time. Tracey was a very easy baby. Our little family of 4 was doing pretty well and we all were happy as little clams.

Since Terry and Tracey were so close in age, they didn't really know a time that they weren't together. After Tracey started school and the first time came that Terry didn't go in because he was sick, Tracey announced that she was staying home too. Of course, we didn't let her. Tracey always felt more secure when Terry was with her. She never wanted to sleep away from home at a friend's house either. And on the rare occasion that she did, we just waited patiently until the parents called us to come and get her. And they always did. She would have what she called 'a feeling' and wanted to be at home with us.

Little Terry would come home from school some days and tell me that Tracey had to come into his class because she was having 'a feeling'. Back then in their little country school, the teachers appeased her and let Tracey come sit by him until she felt comfortable. They were always as close as any two siblings that I have ever known.

What I recall about myself in those early years of marriage, and even after having children, is that I had the 'best little girl in the world' syndrome. I always thought I was just a perfectionist, but now I can look back and see that it was more like perfectionism on steroids! Or as I have come to think of it – as not looking for perfection at all, but looking for what wasn't perfect all the time! Whichever way you look at it, it's exhausting.

I tried to look my best all the time and I tried to keep our home perfectly clean and always in order. What I have come to understand is that being a 'control freak' actually comes from feelings of not having control at all.

We try to control life when we are afraid of losing someone too. But just as squeezing a tiny bird in your hand so they won't fly away may actually kill it – holding on too tightly to someone we love can also kill a relationship.

Eating disorders, alcoholism, and OCD behavior all fall in line with feelings of having no control in your life. So you try to control your surroundings, and even what you eat and drink, and what everyone around you is doing as well.

What I now understand is that while you are trying to keep 'all the plates spinning in the air', you are actually missing out on any type of quality life. And what is actually happening is an unraveling that you aren't noticing.

I didn't know at the time that my behavior was the symptom of my control issues, or lack thereof. I do remember a time that my mother-in-law came to our house for coffee and some sugar spilled on the table and little Terry, who was only around 2 at the time, walked by and stopped to clean up the mess. WOW right?

I was so concerned that everything look perfect all the time that poor little Terry developed an eye twitch. Our pediatrician Dr. Eddie, who had been my own childhood pediatrician, told me to lighten up on him because I was making him nervous! WOW. That was a sad thing to have to accept. But I'm glad Dr. Eddie gave me that wake-up call!

Another time that my excessive compulsion to have everything in order was evident was when a friend offered to watch my daughter Tracey while I did some errands. I dropped Tracey off at Judy's house and Judy had all of her cupboards emptied and on the counters because she was replacing the shelf liners. Judy told me that as soon as I left, Tracey told her that she would help Judy clean everything up before I got back. WOW again! And I know, right?

And yet I still didn't/couldn't stop the feeling that everything must be in its place. I was very lucky to have been able to recognize and tame this malady eventually before it destroyed us. But the control issue thingy is a real thing and is very strong and hard to conquer. This is because as soon as you try to 'let go'- the panic creeps in and the cycle repeats.

Thank goodness I overcame the feeling that everything must be perfect at all times. In fact, I joke now that I can write my name in the dust on my tables and just laugh about it! Although I have to admit that I still do like my house to be tidy and I make up our bed up every morning. I know. I know. I still have some lingering issues.

We never know how our behavior is affecting everyone else while we are suffering from the monkey-talk that we are hearing in our minds. I know it's not a funny thing to laugh at, and I wish I could tell the people who suffer from this that it's alright to mess up sometimes and to loosen up as well. But we all have to come to our own discoveries, at our own pace and time. Sadly, some never do overcome their neuroses and hang-ups, and it can truly ruin relationships.

Another thing that I can share about not realizing how we may be harming our relationships with those closest to us, is that sometimes we speak to friends and co-workers better than we do to our spouses and children. Shouldn't we be speaking more kindly and lovingly to our own family members? They are the ones who put up with us every day. So I vote yes!

Remember that just because our family is supposed to love us...... doesn't mean that they always like us. And even loved ones can find that they've had enough if they are treated poorly enough times. It reminds me of the saying that goes, "Don't push a loyal person so far that they no longer care anymore".

CHAPTER 8

Life on the Farm

When Tracey was about 2 years old, my husband Terry decided that he wanted us to live in the country to raise our children. I don't know how he found the place, but he came home one day and informed me that he had bought me a house. I told him that we already had a house, but he insisted that I would just love it. Rut Roh!

Terry and two of his hunting buddy's, brothers Larry and Squeaky, went in together and bought 80 acres, way out in the country. And I do mean waaaaaay out. Terry sure did love the country life. He said it reminded him of many fond memories in the wooden cabin in Pennsylvania when he was a boy, hunting with his Dad and his Pap Pap.

We split up the 80 acres, and since we had put more money in for the down payment, it was agreed that we would get the 6 bedroom house on the property. There was a smaller house on the other side of the creek too that the brothers agreed Squeaky would get. This was because Larry still lived in Fort Lauderdale with his family. Eventually, everyone had a large home on the property and we all lived there happily for years.

There was another friend who had hunted with the guys and worked with William's brothers too, who eventually lived on the property in a mobile home. There was Richard, Dianne, and their daughter Noel. Their son Shane was born after they moved there permanently. We were all good friends and many nights we women would make all the fixins' and the guys would BBQ, and the brothers would play musical instruments and we all had an old-fashioned country good time.

As John Denver so beautifully sang, ♪♪ 'Life ain't nothing but a funny, funny riddle. Thank God I'm a country boy!' ♪♪

We would have bond fires and marshmallow roasts, and sit out by the creek at night and listen to music, and just visit with each other. The kids would all be sitting around the fire pit with us, or dancing to the music and having fun too. These were much simpler times and I can honestly say that they were some of the best times ever.

Since there was no city water connected to the house, we had to get our water from a well. The well water was briny (salty from leeching in from the nearby creek), and it had a sulfur stench to it too. So, to say that it smelled pretty bad is a huge understatement. I could cook with it and do the laundry, but drinking it was out of the question. So I would haul 8 to 10 five gallon water jugs up to the Franklin Locks, about 5 miles down the road, and fill them up with good drinking water. It made me think of how my grandma in Italy had to haul all of the water they used back in her day.

The kids would play on the playground equipment while I filled the water jugs at the Locks. It was a little break for them, and we did it about 3 or 5 times a week. Sometimes I would go when they were in school, but they really liked going with me so they could enjoy the playground.

I feel that my children had a better life growing up than what I see sometimes in families today, where everyone is on some electronic device and not talking to each other or sharing stories about their day.

After a few years, Terry and I decided that we wanted a third child. Our friend Dianne Carter, who lived in the mobile home on our property, said that she and Richard wanted another child too, and said that if I got pregnant that she would as well. We made a pact that we would get pregnant and then our babies would have each other to play with, and she and I would have each other to share those mom times with.

Well, I can't say for sure if my friend just didn't believe that I would get pregnant, as we had made a pact about, but I did get pregnant right away.......and she didn't. I suspect that she waited until she was sure that I was pregnant before she got pregnant. She had Shane a month after we had Tiffany. They did end up being great company for each other and she and I spent many days together raising our children and playing cards, or Scrabble, and having many family dinners together.

The kids went to the little country school down the road in Alva, and they all did very well. Our girls were always good in school. Tracey was tested for the Gifted Program because the teachers suspected that she had a high I.Q. They were right, and she was placed in the advanced program at her school. And she loved it. Tracey has always been a lover of education and of travel.

I think the quote about the best education is obtained through travel was meant for my Tracey. Tracey has always been enamored with travel. She even bought her own children a globe one year that tells about each country when you wave the pointer over each region. On second thought, maybe the globe was really for her. LOL

When it was time for Tiffany to start school, Tracey had taught her a lot already. Tracey would always be the 'teacher' when they played school in their playroom at home. Tiff was so advanced when she started kindergarten, that when they tested her, her I.Q. test said that she was 11 years and 7 months old, even though she was really only 6 years old.

So Tiffany was put in the Gifted Program as well. They had wanted her to skip a grade and go right into first grade, but her Dad and I thought it would be better that she was always ahead of the class rather than always trying to keep up. We were right. She always excelled in school.

Terry, on the other hand couldn't give a flip about school. I used to joke that I couldn't take all the credit for how well the girls did in school, but I'd be damned if I would take all the blame for Terry's grades. He always passed, but it was with a lot of hair-pulling – mine mostly. But he proved later on, that even though not everyone loves 'book-learnin', they can still excel in life as long as they are doing what they love. And he sure did that!

Life was good on the 'farm'. I say farm, but I was anything but a farm girl. The other women would laugh at me because I would make sure my fingernails and my toenails were always painted and my hair and makeup was always just so. Kinda like Eva Gabor in the TV show Green Acres – but without the million dollars.

One year I tried to plant a garden and it was doing pretty good. That is until one day I watered it with the sprinklers my 'plumbing adept' husband had rigged up for me with water from the creek. Turns out that the county had sprayed the creek for water hyacinths so the creek would flow….and poof, my little garden went bye-bye. I was crushed! But we did get some of the idiot-proof vegetables that I had planted before they were poisoned. Like radishes, pole beans, summer squash, etc. They are called idiot-proof because anyone can grow them. No offense taken. And I was pretty proud of my little garden….while it lasted.

Another attempt at being a farm wife was when I tried to raise chickens to lay eggs. I just couldn't understand why the chickens were pecking each other's eyes out! YIKES right? I didn't know that there is a 'pecking' order (not a pun), and that you may just have a bully in the hen house.

I had spent a fortune on feed and drops and had even put marbles in the water that were supposed to fool the chickens, I guess, into thinking they were eyeballs! I finally just let them all out of the chicken coop. They went over to my friend Kay's house eventually. I figured that if I ever did get eggs out of them, I estimated that it would have cost me about $20.00 a dozen! So I just bought eggs from other REAL farm wives in the area. But those little 'biddies' (baby chicks) sure were cute!

I also had a problem raising rabbits. Yeah, rabbits! Can you imagine? Everyone always says how rabbits multiply…..well, like rabbits. But MY rabbits? They ate their babies. I gave up!

The information given on the internet about 'Raising Rabbits' is: [Rabbits are prey animals that exist at the bottom of the hierarchy. In the rabbit's perspective, everything out there has a huge set of fangs or a very sharp beak, along with a very big appetite. But that doesn't mean it just gives itself up and lays down on the dinner plate. The doe rabbit does all she can to personally survive and keep having babies for the good of the species].

But I found out that some rabbits don't have the same motherly instinct of protecting their babies. No kidding Sherlock!

We also decided to just buy our beef rather than try to raise it since we hadn't had much success in the farm-type endeavors we had tried before. It was just too easy to buy a half or a quarter of a cow from one of the other farm families. We had it cut to the specifications we wanted and it was wrapped and labeled. Easy Peasy and I didn't have to try my hand at cattle ranching! I don't even want to think how that could have ended.

We had a PO Box at the post office up by the river. Right next door was the Alva Country & Supply Store, owned by Betty and Jack. It was like a 7-11, only very countrified. You could buy lunchmeats, milk, bread, and most anything you might have run out of before you could get back to the big grocery store, which was about 25 miles away. Betty & Jack's had 2 old-fashioned gas pumps out in front of the store, and it always reminded me of Ike Godsey's store from The Walton's TV show.

The in and out screen doors at the little country store would open and slam shut quite a bit, as customers came and went. This meant that Betty and Jack were doing OK. But Betty and Jack were not very gabby people, especially to out-of-towners. They were skeptical of us when we all moved into the area. City folk, don't you know? But we were very good customers, so they abided us. Most times the kids would get a candy bar and a cold drink when we went in to buy some groceries, and the kids were usually in bare feet. Guess they got that from their Mom.

We didn't eat dinner out very often, but there was a restaurant called Marina 31 about 10 miles up the road that we would go to once or twice a year. The kids really thought that was a treat. Kids these days go out so often that they don't think it's anything big or special at all. I really think that's why the children of today's generation are easily bored. They have so much crammed into their short lives that they expect to be amused every second of their waking hours. And they have no clue how to entertain themselves like we did back then.

Another big whoop in our country-life was that once a year there was the Swamp Cabbage Festival in LaBelle to look forward to. And I'm not being snarky here at all. It was a very big deal and we all looked forward to going.

The Swamp Cabbage Festival is always the last full weekend in February. You will find anything from armadillo races to eating the most delicious Pumpkin Bread that is made and sold by the Seminole Indian women at the event. The festival had everything from teenage girls in beauty pageants, and the high school band playing in the parade, to live entertainment by the locals, to a fishing tournament, and much more family fun stuff. And the big entertainment was the rodeo.

The most interesting thing about the festival to me was that since it's strictly a family affair, no alcoholic beverages were sold there....back in the day anyway! Whoa....right? But these 'Florida Crackers' had a lot of fun and were proud of their heritage. And 'Florida Cracker' is not meant as a putdown of any sort. The term just refers to the colonial-era English and American pioneer settlers and their descendants who settled in what is now known as Florida.

Swamp cabbage is actually called hearts of palm when you pay big bucks for it in a fancy restaurant. It comes from the inside of the state tree, the sabal or cabbage palm. It tastes pretty much like regular cabbage, and it tastes mighty good when you cook it with some pork fat.

The Caloosahatchee River ran alongside the general store and you could see kids jumping off into the river most any time you rode over the bridge or visited the store. I can't swear that my kids never jumped from there, but I wouldn't be surprised if they did. But they did have plenty to do at home. Cypress Creek ran right through our acreage, and the kids would jump into the creek from a long rope hanging from a big old oak tree. Or they would just fish off the dock that their Dad had built. They also rode their 3-Wheelers all around the property.

I also remember the most gorgeous sunsets imaginable on the West Coast. The sun would reflect in red-blood splendor on the river as it said goodnight to the day. No artist could ever paint a sky as beautiful as Mother Nature displayed to us for free! And the thunder and lightning 'shows' were incredible as well. That area of the West Coast of Florida is known as the lightning capitol of North America.

I remember a time that my Dad was sitting in our den and a lightning bolt hit a palm tree right outside by where he was sitting. My Dad was wearing a cap at the time, and when we went in to see if he was ok, he tried to take off his hat, and it was stuck to his hair! That was a close one for sure. We looked out the window and the palm tree had imploded from the lightning strike, and there was not much left of it. It looked like it had been bombed, from the inside.

On another day, little Terry was fishing from the dock and he caught a catfish. When he tried to retrieve the hook from its mouth, the catfish chomped down and Terry started yelling. Tracey ran up to the house screaming that the fish was eating Terry! We didn't know if it was an alligator or what! Big Terry raced down to the creek and he carefully got Terry's finger out of the catfish's mouth and all was well. Just another day on the 'farm'.

The creek that I mentioned didn't have a way to get to the other side without going out onto the road, so the men decided to build a bridge. They were very ingenious and used water hoses to 'dig' holes in the muddy creek bottom to anchor the posts. The posts were creosote coated utility poles, like the ones that are used for power lines and telephone poles.

After the posts were stabilized in the creek bottom, the guys started laying the wood across sideways and then long ways. Then they built a shingle roof for the top. When it was finished, we had a lovely covered bridge to walk or drive across to the other side of the creek, much like the kind you would see in the movie The Bridges of Madison County.

It took a while to build and we women would bring our lawn chairs out and watch, while we drank our sweet tea and brought some to the men too, since they were working so hard. The kids would all play hide and seek or tag and have a dip in the creek while their Dad's worked on the bridge.

Even though it was a lot of work, the men had fun building it. They were all a bunch of young and fit guys who were friends too, and they enjoyed hanging out together, even if that meant building bridges – literally and figuratively. Hey, that's a pretty sweet metaphor!

When the men were finished for the day, we women would fix supper, and a lot of the time we would have a cookout and we'd all eat together. Then we would go to our respective homes, watch a little TV, bathe, and hit the sack.

We only had one TV and it was in the family room. What a concept eh? One TV in one room, instead of like today, where there is one in every room in the house!

The TV only received 2 channels fairly well, and one other channel, if and when it decided to show up. The cloudier the skies, the better the third channel would come in. There were no remotes (unless you count telling the kids to get up and change channels). Ha!

It was funny when we first moved there because the local channels would have news like – "Miss Sarah will be having an ice cream social this Sunday on her porch after church and everyone is invited – or, the Jones family lost their pet pig Susie, and if anyone finds her, they'd appreciate you bringing her home to them - and not eating her."

We were all very easily entertained. No doubt, right? But it was a sweet and uncomplicated time and place to live and to raise a family. And I'm grateful that we did choose to move to the country to raise our children. Well, that Terry decided to move us to the country to raise our family anyway. LOL

My friend Kay, who was on the same side of the creek as us, was what I considered a real country lady. She was from Louisiana and she was a very good person. Kay taught me how to sew and how to make jams and jellies and how to can vegetables. Let me clarify the sewing part. Kay TRIED to teach me how to sew. I just didn't have the knack I guess. Kay told me it relaxed her, but I never found that to be true for me. By the time I was finished with an item, my shoulders would be as tight as a tick on a hound. Kay and I became very close friends.

Kay was typical of Southern understatement. She was also the 180 opposite of my 'Yankee' way of dealing with any crisis. I joked once that if the house was on fire, Kay would probably calmly say something like, "We should maybe go outside because there seems to be some smoke filling up the house". I, on the other hand.....would probably go screaming out the door. I admit that I've never been very good in a crisis.

As Richard Bach offered about friends: "The bond that links your true family is not one of blood, but of respect and joy in each other's life. Rarely do members of one family grow up under the same roof." And we were a family of friends for sure. Another quote I love about friends is by Robert Southey, "No distance of place, or lapse of time, can lessen the friendship of those who are thoroughly persuaded of each other's worth".

We also had a friend who owned tomato fields and he would sell the best of his crop off and then he would sell to the vegetable pinhookers, who sell mainly to small restaurants and individuals. And then he would sell to the guys who peddle tomatoes out of the backs of their trucks that you see on the side of the road. After all that, Stancil Taylor would let us come in and pick whatever we wanted - - for free. And there was plenty left for us.

The problem with free – and yes there really can be a problem with free – is that your eyes and your intentions can be bigger than your ability to 'can' all you pick. We picked so many tomatoes one time that our fingers cracked open from canning so many of the acidic vegetables.

Another time we got so many green beans that our kids wouldn't even come inside to go to the bathroom for fear that we'd make them sit down and snap some beans with us! And we did make them snap with us for sure because we had A LOT of beans. Thank goodness that Child Labor Laws were not in force in our home! I canned 128 quarts of string beans myself that year for our family.

Another year we overloaded ourselves with corn. I guess we were slow learners or just had bad memories of all the work that lay ahead of us. But the truth about the corn is that my husband had stopped in Immokalee (a town known for vegetable picking and shipping) and brought home crates and crates of corn in their shucks. So, we couldn't let it go to waste. Whatever we didn't finish canning that day, we'd have it for dinner. We ate a lot of corn and green beans I tell ya'.

The top of our cabinets in our large farm kitchen were loaded with the jars of vegetables and jams and jellies that I had canned. Big Terry always worried that the cabinets would fall off the walls from all the weight. But that never happened, and we always had lots of healthy stuff to eat. And it was yummy too!

Life was pretty good all around. My mom would come over from Hollywood almost every weekend. Dad would only come occasionally. Many of our 'city' friends would come to visit for the weekend too. Our 6 bedroom house could hold a lot of guests. Big Terry's mom and dad, and Grandma Nell and Pap Pap would come a few times a year, especially for the birthdays. Terry's brothers and sisters would also come up often to visit us. One of Terry's brothers Tim, and a friend name Fred even moved into our barn and made a bedroom in the loft area. We were all just one big happy family.

I often think that children may not remember every warm and fuzzy adventure they experienced growing up with the family, but they do know how good it felt to be surrounded by love. I sense those experiences are 'baked' into their psyche's and it forms who they will always be as grown adults. It's like the saying that you can take the girl/boy out of the country, but you can't take the country out of the girl/boy. And that's the same for wherever we were brought up. I know that city kids have their warm and fuzzy memories baked into their consciousness as well!

Big Terry would make the trip over to Hollywood for business meetings sometimes, and it would just be the kids and me at home until he returned.

Then when Terry was 12 and Tracey was 11 and Tiffany was 8 …….everything in our lives changed after one of his trips. Drastically. And Forever!

CHAPTER 9

Life Happens When You Are Making Other Plans

A knock on our door woke us up very early in the morning on April 1st, 1983. I opened the door to find a sheriff deputy standing there with a very serious look on his face. I couldn't imagine what he could want with us. I remember thinking that he couldn't want us for anything related to the law. A number of things do go racing through your mind at times like these. I thought maybe one of our cows or horses had gotten out again. But I could also sense that the last thing in the world that this young deputy seemed to want at that moment, was to be looking at a young woman and her 3 children staring back at him with the news that he did have for us.

He then asked me if there was anyone I could call to be with me. And at that moment I felt a sickening feeling in the pit of my stomach. I knew then that something was very, very, terribly wrong. I said why, what's wrong? He didn't answer right away so I asked again. What's wrong?

He then asked once more if there was someone I could call. That's when I screamed WHAT'S WRONG....TELL ME!!!!! He said, "I'm very sorry ma'am but your husband was in a car accident last night." Then I asked him, no I hoped and prayed, is he ok? There was a silence that seemed like it lasted for hours. Then he looked downward, I guess because it was too hard to look me in the eyes, and he finally said, "No ma'am. I'm sorry but he's gone."

I remember gasping, and then trying to suck air back into my lungs, as the kids were all crying and clinging to me. It felt as if time was being suspended in some sort of weird way. I didn't know what to do or say, so I just stared at him in disbelief. He asked if I would like him to stay until someone could come to be with us. But I said no thank you. And he left.

It was awful. Just awful. No, it was unimaginable. Why Terry? Why was he taken so young? What could have possibly happened? What were we going to do? And what were the kids going to do without a Dad? It was too much for us to take in or to grasp at that moment.

As if in a crazed kind of stupor, I somehow got word to our friends who lived on the property, and they and Terry's brother Tim came over and we just sat there crying in shock. This couldn't be true. It just couldn't. But it was.....

The fear of what was going to happen in our lives without him and the fear of how the children were going to get through this filled me with terror. I kept feeling like I was in some kind of crazy time warp, or trapped in the middle of a nightmare. I kept seeing Terry's face and hearing his voice. I went to his closet and smelled his clothes. I kept praying that this was all just a very bad dream, and that I would wake up and everything would be just like it was before that awful knock on our door.

Later on in the day, I remember going to Terry's closet again; but this time I was picking out a suit, shirt, dress shoes, underwear and socks for him. All as if I were in a trance. I don't know how or why, but I just knew to bring his things with us, and any paperwork that I thought I may need for the drive over to Hollywood, where his body was being kept until I could decide on funeral arrangements.

People have told me over the years what a strong person I am. But the truth is that you don't have a choice when awful things happen to you. You either 'handle' what happens or you crumble. I do believe we are all much stronger than we think we are. But I now had to face the fact that I belonged to a sad, sad 'club' of widows, of which no one would ever want to be a member.

What had happened is that Terry had just met with some friends on the East Coast of Florida. It was about 9 PM when he finished his visit. He was on his way to spend the night at my mom's house. And he had an appointment for a meeting with our family attorney the following day for some business.

He was driving on a two-lane road and the front tire on his car got caught in a rut on the side of the road. He over-corrected the car and hit a line of Australian Pine trees on the opposite side of the road. It turned out that the pedals on his car were too close together and when he thought he was pressing on the brake, the accelerator was being pressed as well, and the car accelerated instead, and his car careened into the line of tall trees.

They told me that Terry was killed instantly from blunt trauma to the side of his head. Someone told me later that a nice person must have heard the crash and came to put a blanket over Terry. I've always been saddened at the thought that he was all by himself when he died. But I know that Terry would never have wanted us to be with him when the accident happened. He loved his family more than life itself and wouldn't have wanted us to be harmed in any way.

Terry was an excellent driver and I never in a million years would have ever expected him to die in a car accident, in which he was the driver. As I mentioned earlier, Terry had driven Stock Cars, so he knew how to handle himself behind the wheel of a car.

You couldn't even see any marks on his body at the funeral, and I was so grateful for that. And I was thankful that the children, his Mom and Dad, brothers and sisters, and friends were able to remember him the way he always looked. He looked like he was just sleeping peacefully in his casket, and as handsome as ever.

It was all very, very sad as you can imagine. All of his friends, young and old, came to his funeral. And he had a lot of friends too. When we die when we're old, there aren't many friends left to come to your funeral, but when you're only 34, everyone is still around and they come to pay their respects and show their love. And he was loved by so many, many people!

There were many decisions to be made about what the kids and I would do, but I wasn't able to make any decisions right then. I've since heard that you should never make any big decisions right after a tragedy and that it's best to wait a full year before making life-changing decisions about the future. And we had had enough changes to our life already.

Going back home to the 'farm' a few days after the funeral was surreal. It didn't feel like home anymore without Terry there. I didn't feel safe anymore. I don't mean the kind of safe where you fear for your safety, or that someone will break into your home or anything. It was the safe feeling I had taken for granted when our family was whole. When we were a unit.....when we were together. When feeling intact was a given. But I found out that nothing is a given. And that feeling can be taken away instantaneously.

The realities of life don't give you any breaks when it comes to 'going on' after a tragic loss. I did have to get a job. And it wasn't a very easy commute since we lived 25 miles from any big town or city. But I did get a position as a hairdresser in Fort Myers. I would drive the 25 miles to and from work, and the kids would have to look after themselves after school for a few hours until I got home. I didn't have many options, and we did what we had to do. They were really good kids and I don't know what I would have done without their help. We were there for each other, and the circumstances that we found ourselves in made us even closer, if that was possible.

The girls would clean the house for me and Terry would use our small Ford tractor to mow the grass that was just around the house. I didn't want him to drive the big tractor because it was too dangerous for any kid to operate. Especially if I wasn't at home.

But life still had to go on. There were the usual lunches to make for school and dinners to cook and then the laundry to get done and hang out on the line, and bring it back in when it was dry. And there was all that damn grass that had to be mowed.

We had an old, and I do mean old, Massey Ferguson tractor with a bush hog on the back. You had to put hydraulic fluid in it every time you mowed because it had a small leak somewhere. I remember looking like I had reverse raccoon eyes when I would get off the tractor. I would wear sunglasses while I mowed, and when I took them off, the area behind them was the only white parts left on my face. I swear sometimes I could hear that grass growing as I fell asleep at night. I felt just like the commercial about the groggy donut maker – 'It's time to make the donuts again.' But for me it was, it's time to mow the damn grass again.

I tried to hang in there for about a year and then I had to give up. The kids didn't want to leave their home but it was killing me. I just couldn't do it anymore. After a time, I sold the house and my share of the acreage. A group of retired nuns bought it as a retirement home. I just heard recently that they still live there, all these many years later. Turns out that awesome place is a good choice for a peaceful retirement in addition to raising a family.

So we moved back to Hollywood to be closer to family. Mine and Terry's. I rented a house and got the kids settled into their respective schools. Then I went to work as a hostess at Terry's parent's restaurant and raw bar on the Intracoastal side of A1A, in Hollywood Beach.

I do have to say that all of the kids sure did citify up quickly. I know they missed the farm life, but they acclimated to their new normal very fast. Children are amazingly resilient and my three handled what was left of their life like champions.

This was our new normal now. It may sound as if our life was tied up in a neat little bow then – but it felt nothing like a gift. But we did try to live normal lives. Whatever 'normal' meant to us now.

CHAPTER 10

Starting Over – AGAIN

Little Terry went to a Catholic School at Chaminade and played football there too. Tracey also went to a Catholic school, Little Flower, and Tiffany went to a public elementary school. I was not Catholic, but their Dad was and I decided that those schools were the best choices for each of them at the ages they were. Days melted into weeks and then months and then a year. But our lives were never the same again. Never.

After a while, I started going out with the gang from the raw bar where I worked. They were a bunch of great friends and we did have fun. Dating was a far-off notion to me, but going out with the gang was always a good time, and something to do with grownups.

Then I met Mike. Mike had just recently moved into the area from Chicago. He is really from Memphis but had been working in Chicago and had been offered a managerial position at Farm Stores, and had relocated to Miami.

Mike was living in an apartment by the beach and would come into the Dockside Raw Bar with his bicycle cop friend Sandy. They would come in often and we would chat and joke around. One day he said to Sandy that if I, meaning me, wasn't married, he'd sure like to ask me out. He assumed that I was married because I was still wearing my wedding rings.

Sandy told him that I wasn't married and that I was a widow. So one day he did ask me out. I said yes to a date and we planned to go to the Le Tub restaurant the next night. Le Tub is a restaurant right next to the restaurant where I was working.

Well, the next night I got to Le Tub and there was no Mike. I thought it was a bit rude of him, but I figured it was no biggie. There was no attachment yet between us, so I just went back home. But the next time he came into the Dockside, everyone gave him the cold shoulder, and when he asked what was wrong, they told him they couldn't believe that he had stood me up. He swore that he didn't think I was serious about meeting him. So I forgave him.

We met in April and were married the following December. I guess you could say that I really did forgive him. Or did I? Ha!

Let me tell you all right now that blended families are not for the faint of heart. By the time Mike and I married, the kids were 15, 14 and 10. Terry and Tracey didn't want anything to do with Mike at first. Only little Tiffany really did very much with him at all. Mike had a son, Mikey, who was 2 ½ at the time and Tiffany just loved him to bits. We all did. He was just the cutest and most animated little boy! Terry and Tracey were good with Mikey too and they even taught him how to swim in the pool at our home that Mike and I had purchased.

It was just Mike that they seemed to have an issue with. And it wasn't even Mike that they minded. I know it could have been anyone who would have come into their lives after they had lost their Dad. And looking back, it is easier to understand now than when we were all going through those times. It's bad enough for kids to adjust when there is a divorce, but when there's a death, it magnifies and upsets the family dynamic on many different levels.

If I could give any advice to blended families, it would be for the parent of the children involved to not allow either the spouse or the children to drag you into their 'fight'. I tried to be everyone's best friend and that just doesn't work. If I took the children's side, Mike felt upset. If took Mike's side, the children felt upset. I should have just said that whoever is having a problem with whomever – to work it out together and leave me out of it. I love you all and I refuse to take sides. Period.

And as I pointed to before, it was not the fault of anyone in particular that our family blending was so hard for us. I just wish I had understood all of this better back then. But.....I didn't.

But Tracey and Mike are fine now. I can say without a doubt that Mike loves Tracey as if she were his very own daughter, and Tracey is so very good to both of us. Mike often remarks how proud he is of Tracey and the wonderful woman, wife, and mother she has become.

Mike never tried to say he was the children's Dad, but he was always there for them and for me. I have told him often that if it had been the other way around and he was a widower with teens, I don't think I could have hung in as well as he did. I would have said for him to give me a call when the last one leaves home. But he did hang in there and eventually - well after about 6 years, and after some iffy times - everything and everyone began to mesh nicely. And then this was our new normal.

So, if there are any blended families out there reading this....don't give up hope. And what I can offer to anyone who may be going through this now is that one day all of the children will have families of their own, and if you and your husband can hang in there, you and he will have each other when everyone leaves you and goes on to live their own life. And if you don't make it work – you will be the one who is left all alone.

I've come to understand that for life to unfold smoothly, it takes a lot of being able to adjust to change. Change is inevitable, and thinking otherwise and going against the flow of life, just brings us more angst and unhappiness.

Mikey came to stay with us in the summers until he was going into the 5th grade. What happened was that Mike, Tracey and I had gone to Chicago to visit him, and after we brought him back to his home for the night, after a day of sight-seeing in downtown Chi-Town, and we had gotten back to our hotel, Mikey called us and told his Dad that he wanted to come and live with him full time. Of course, Mike was thrilled and he eventually worked it out with Mikey's mom. But it was a complicated decision that had to be made.

It was a decision that would take a lot of thought and conversations between my Mike and his ex-wife. But they came to the agreement that as a boy, Mikey needed to be with his Dad at this age. And Mikey had made it very clear that he did want to come down and live with his Dad.

Mikey was always treated like a little king when he had visited us. I used to joke that I wanted to come back as Mikey after I died because he had the best of both worlds. He was loved very much by his mother and Nona and Papa, and other family members when he was in Chicago, and he was loved and adored very much by all of his Florida family and friends when he was with us.

So they switched custody times, and Mikey stayed with us for the school year and went to stay with his mom in the summers. I always made sure to keep Mikey's Mom in the loop about anything that was going on in his life. I made sure she got school pictures and copies of his report cards, and all things pertaining to him. I never had any problems with Mike's ex-wife for 30 something years. I feel it was because I always took her feelings into consideration, the way I would have wanted to be treated if it were my children who were living away from me for a time.

Mike and I gave Mikey the best private, parochial schooling for the rest of his grade school and high school years. I can still remember starching and ironing his school uniforms. He looked like a young professional at the breakfast table with his white, starched shirt and his school tie and blazer.

I would always put the sports section of the paper by his orange juice, toast and cereal each morning. Then we'd be off to take him to school. I'd also wait in the drive-up line to pick him up each afternoon when school let out. Mikey has always had the sort of personality that he always made friends fast and he did well in school.

I have to say that step-parents get a bad rap a lot of the time. But when you think about it, step-parents do for and love their step-children because they WANT to, not because they HAVE to.

Mikey always joked that he had a penthouse apartment in our home in Tennessee. He had the entire top floor to himself, which included a huge sitting room with a giant TV. He and his friends had many good times up there just hanging out.

We surprised Mikey with a cool VW Bug on his sixteenth birthday. It was shiny blue and he was ecstatic when he saw it in the driveway! We later bought him a Ford Edge truck when we moved back to Florida again. We hadn't even done that for my own children. They had had to buy their own cars.

Mike was working about 50 miles from home when we lived in Tennessee. We had bought another small house on the golf course and Mikey and I would go out and spend from Friday night until Sunday evening at the course. This was our life until Mikey graduated from high school and started going to The University of Memphis.

Previous to this, when we lived in Florida, and after Mike and I had gotten married, we had opened a raw bar restaurant in Davie, Florida. We named it Brady's Raw Bar and Grille. Mike stayed working at his managerial position at Farm Stores and did double-duty with shifts at the restaurant. He finally left the Farm Stores job and we switched off with our work shifts at Brady's. Each of us either worked the day or night shifts at the restaurant. One of us was mostly there all the time.

We didn't see much of each other during our restaurant owning days. We would tell each other what had gone on during our respective shifts, and anything the other one of us needed to know, and then one would leave to go home, and the other would work their shift at the restaurant.

Things were good at the restaurant and Mike was a big part of bringing in customers. He played in several softball leagues. He was on 5 teams at once! But the good part is that after the games, Mike offered the winning team 3 free pitchers of beer with their food order. And the losing team would get 2 free pitchers of beer with their order. The whole teams and their families would pile in after their game. We would turn the tables with softball players and their families a couple of times a night.

Our crew at the restaurant were the best of the best. Dockside had closed by then and we got a lot of the staff that had worked there. Even the head cooks! It felt like family. My girls worked there too and everyone loved them. Even little Mikey helped out in the summers when he used to come down for his visits with us. I can still see him standing on a chair in the back area of the restaurant, helping the bussers with the dishwashing, while wearing an apron that was way too big for him. But later in life, he has told his Dad that we taught him a good work ethic. So, I guess that we weren't so bad after all.

Mikes' niece and nephews worked there for us too, as did Tracey and Tiffany. As I said, it was a family affair for sure! The customers all felt like family too and we had a good run with it until the 1990 Iraq war, 'Operation Desert Storm' broke out.

Every night the war and the repercussions of the Kuwait invasion was being shown on TV. The economy was tanking as people were afraid of what was to come, and they didn't feel much like spending money, never mind eating out. So we decided to get rid of the restaurant business in 1991. The strip mall we were in was supposed to be torn down for another venue anyway, so it was a good time to make a life change.

If anyone ever says they want to own a restaurant, try to dissuade them. It is a grueling life of many long hours - 24/7 and 365 days a year. We did make a lot of great friends while we owned the restaurant, but it was tremendously hard on our relationship and family life. Wait.....what family life?

We sold our restaurant equipment to Arrowhead Golf and Country Club, that former football legend Earl Morrall owned, and started working for him at his club. Earl was a great guy! One of the best football players ever (he was the quarterback for the 1972 Miami Dolphins' undefeated season) and more importantly, he was just very a kind, decent, and humble family man.

Mike and I have had the opportunity to meet many former great NFL and MLB and even a few NHL players, and they were very good people. At least the ones we were involved within our charity work.

I was the beverage cart 'girl' and Mike was the Manager at Arrowhead Country Club. It was a nice change from working the different shifts and so many hours at our own restaurant. And for a change, we had some of our nights off together. And it was great to not have to worry about business once we got home. Ownership has a lot of perks, but just being an employee is kind of nice too, especially after having been a restaurant owner with the grueling hours that go with it.

Things were going well. Terry (LT) was in the Army and then he and Deana were married. And Terry was making us all very proud of his accomplishments while he was in the Army.

Everyone is given a nickname in the military, and since his last name was (Pribisco), and sounded like Nabisco, they gave him the nickname - Biscuit. Terry continued with the tradition by giving that nickname to his son as well when Terry #3....uh, little Biscuit was born.

Terry achieved the awesome accomplishment of becoming an Army Airborne Ranger during his time of service. "The United States Army Rangers are an elite rapid-deployment military formation of the Army".

Becoming a Ranger is one of the hardest achievements to attain in the military. And Terry did it with flying colors. Terry was never one to love school, but he sure did excel when it came to being in the Army. He received many honors, one of which was Sharp-Shooter during his time in the Army. I guess all those hunting years on the farm paid off.

He decided to get out of the Army when his duty was over, and we were very happy to have him home with us again. He and Deana were pregnant with their daughter Megan by then.

I think being a Gommy at a young age has its perks because you are young enough to fully enjoy your little grands, and all that it takes to keep up with them. I was a young mom too and a very young Gommy, and I am now a kinda' youngish Great Gommy to Megan's sweet little Henry.

Terry and Deana were expecting their daughter Megan in October. Tracey had just received her undergraduate degree from the University of Miami and Tiffany was going to graduate soon and go to U of M too. Everything in life was going beautifully. And then tragedy struck us again!

CHAPTER 11

The Shattering Suffering Continues

Then the unimaginable and unfathomable happened. AGAIN! Tracey and I had been shopping and when we got home, I called my Mom. There were no cell phones back then so we had to wait until we got home to use the landline. When I called Mom, she told me that Terry and Tiffany had been in an accident. Mom seemed eerily calm, which was very unusual when it was about something that pertained to her grandchildren being in any sort of harm's way.

I immediately got that sick feeling in the pit of my gut again. But I thought that there's no way this could be happening again. I had just spoken to them that very morning. They were on their way over to see Terry's brand new baby girl Megan. The last thing I said to Tiff was to call when they got there safely and to be careful and that I loved her and Terry. I told her to tell Deana that Tracey and I would be over to see her and Megan in a few days. Then we hung up saying our usual I love you's.

I asked Mom if they were ok. She quietly said, "They're gone". I didn't think I had heard her right because she sounded so uncharacteristically calm about something so horrific. I said what do you mean they're gone? I remembered the last time I had heard the word 'gone' like that, and how our lives were changed forever after hearing it. Then Mom said, "They are dead Shirley."

There was a lot of screaming and crying from Tracey and me as you might imagine. We just clung to each other in disbelief. Again. How could this be happening over and over again? It was more than surreal. It was sickening. And it was deeper than any shock imaginable!

Tiffany had been driving her car at the time of the accident, and all I can think of when I think of the accident now is that Mack truck hitting them. And try as I may, I can't seem to un-see it. All these years later.

They said there was debris all over, and some of the items were gifts that Terry and Tiffy were taking over for baby Megan. There was even a stroller in the trunk. The only consolation that I have is that they were together and not alone when they died.

Mike was working in the Memphis area at the time, and I called him. The woman who answered the phone went outside to find Mike and told him that he better call me because I was screaming and crying so loudly that she couldn't understand anything I had said. Her name was Willie and I can only imagine how upset Willie must have been, to have to tell Mike to call me back. She knew it had to be something horrifyingly dreadful by the way I was screaming. And it was.

When Mike called back, I told him what had happened. He immediately called our forever friend Richard and asked him to pick my Mom up on the way and to come over and stay with Tracey and me until he could get back. Mike made arrangements to fly back immediately.

This time I really was in total and absolute shock, and so was Tracey. Tracey and I went to the beach that night just to be alone together. We didn't say much. Words weren't necessary for the feelings that we were sharing. It was just important to be with each other. I can't even explain in words how much everything just seemed empty and unreal. I felt empty and I know Tracey felt empty too. She had lost her dad when she was just a little girl and now she had lost her best friends in her big brother and her little sister. This much pain isn't supposed to happen to one family. But it did happen. And it kept happening to us.

I remember laying on my bed, crying….no I was sobbing. I just couldn't do this again. How do you bury your children? They had so much more life to share with us. I kept thinking it was just a horrible nightmare. That is would go away. But it didn't go away.

In time, I came to understand that my Mom's response was one of deep shock as well. My children were the loves of her life. And it was just too much for her to take in.

The next few days were a blur. Thank goodness for my Mom and for Mike. Mom went with us to the funeral home to pick out caskets and make the arrangements for our beautiful boy and girl. I never thought this could ever happen if I had lived to be 100 years old.

After losing my husband Terry at such a young age, I had figured that we'd surely experienced all of the misfortune, death, and sadness for a lifetime. But life had other plans for us.

The funeral for Terry and Tiffany was so big that the police had to put extra detail on to manage the amount of cars that were full of friends and family who came to pay their respects and show their love and respect for both of them.

Tiffany's high school had put on a beautiful ceremony to honor her as well. But I have to admit that that whole time is fuzzy for me. Somehow we managed to attend, but I don't remember much about it, except the other kids and faculty were all crying along with us.

Taps was played for Terry at the gravesite and it was all I could do not to jump into the gravesite holes with them. But Tracey needed me more than ever now. Mike was a tower of strength for us and I am so very grateful for his support and love at such a horrendous time for us to have to get through.

Their gravesites were next to their Dad's – and my Dad, and their great Grandma's Maudie and Great Grandma O'Connell (their Dad's Grandma). And these days, that whole section of the cemetery is full of family members. On both sides of our family.

What author Michael Singer says about death is so very true: "No person or situation could ever teach you as much as death has to teach you. While someone could tell you that you are not your body, death shows you".

When you lose people you love so dearly, life after they are gone is never the same. It's like losing a spoke in a wheel or a thread from a fine tapestry. The wheel may still work and the tapestry is still beautiful....but you will always notice the missing spoke and see where the missing threads are supposed to be.

I had thought that I had had the worst day of my life when my husband died. But burying your children is surely the worst day anyone could ever have in their life. And then, once again, I found myself in another terrible 'club' which no parent would ever want to be a member.

People always say that time heals all wounds and that it gets better – but for me, I think it's more that you learn to manage life with a different normal. But it's a normal that you would never, ever, ever choose if you did have the choice. Ever!

You also have to figure out how you are going to adjust, and how you are going to go on living now that they are gone. I had heard people say that you can become bitter or you can become better, and I chose to be better. It was the only way I could think of to honor their memory. And they certainly deserved to be honored. I know how precious life is and I feel I have an even greater obligation to Terry and Tiffany and their Dad, to enjoy every minute I am given and to appreciate and squeeze out every beautiful ounce that life has to offer - since they didn't get to. Anything else would dishonor their memory. And that would be intolerable.

My perspective about life was changed forever after Terry and Tiffany died. There were a lot of things that I no longer cared about. Like feeling that I had to always 'be right' when that only leads to silly arguments about things that just don't matter. And the million other things that take up useless space in our heads.

But there are a lot of other things that I care even more deeply about than I ever had before. Like enjoying every day that I am allowed to wake up and live another day. Or the precious time I get to spend with family and friends. Death is the ultimate wake-up call that makes us grateful for what we do have, and not give a hill of beans about what we don't have. And death also teaches us in the cruelest possible way, to never take anyone for granted.

I am so very happy that Tracey and I had gone on mother/daughter trips throughout the years. Before Tracey married, she and I went on trips to California, New York City, and Boston. Those times and memories are very special and very precious to me. It's so very heart-warming when your daughter also becomes your best friend.

And I am thankful every morning when we wake up. When Mike gets up from our bed, I place my hand on the place where had slept and feel the warmth left there from his body, and I say thank you for another day to spend with my best friend.

Terry and Tiffany died on October 26, 1992. I remember the next month was Thanksgiving. We didn't really feel that we had anything to be grateful for at the time, but we prepared the Thanksgiving meal and tried to pretend. I know now that we did have much to be grateful for. We still had each other. I cannot imagine people who have to go through such suffering all alone.

It's been over 26 years now since the accident and some days it seems like yesterday and other times it feels like it was a hundred years ago. And some days, I wonder if it really was a nightmare that I haven't awakened from yet.

Then on Terry's next birthday, a newspaper article came out about Tiffany's 'graduation'. A graduation that she would never have. This is the article:

["In Remembrance, Mom Accepts Posthumous High School Diploma For Daughter Killed In 1992 Traffic Accident.

June 16, 1993|By LUCIO GUERRERO, Staff Writer

HOLLYWOOD -- Shirley Pribisco Brady took the hardest walk of her life on Tuesday night, onto a school stage to accept an honorary posthumous high school diploma for her daughter.

Tiffany Pribisco, 17, a senior at South Broward High School, was killed in a traffic accident in October. Her friends and teachers honored her on Tuesday with an honorary diploma during the school's senior awards ceremony.

"This will probably be the hardest night since the accident" Mike Brady, Tiffany's stepfather, said before the ceremony. "When someone gives you a diploma with your child's name on it and she is not here anymore, that's reality".

For the family, it was a double tragedy. Tiffany and her brother, Terry, died in the accident in Hendry County. Today would have been Terry Pribisco's 23rd birthday.

According to police, Tiffany Pribisco lost control of her car after she passed a truck on a rural road. The wheels of the car drifted onto the shoulder, spinning the car out of control and into the path of an oncoming dump truck.

Tiffany was vice president of both the senior class and the student council. She was on her way to Fort Myers with her brother when the accident happened.

Along with the diploma, Shirley Brady and her other daughter, Tracey, received a portrait of Tiffany and a framed cover of the class yearbook, which was dedicated to Tiffany.

The family has started a scholarship fund in honor of Tiffany and Terry for South Broward High students.

Jennifer Wilcox, senior class president and one of Tiffany's closest friends, was fighting tears when she announced that the money left over from the senior budget would be donated to the scholarship".]

Terry had been a decorated member of the military, and excelled greatly and honorably. And Tiffany was the light that lit up every room that she ever entered. They were both extraordinary people. I always say that Tiff was an old soul. I guess that she and Terry were just 'finished' with all of their life's lessons - this go around. If their mission in choosing this life was to fill the hearts of everyone they met with love and compassion, they certainly did accomplish that mission. I was truly blessed with 3 of the most wonderful children a mother could ever have had. Becoming bitter would have seemed to tarnish those blessings. So we went on with life, such as it was.

Mike decided to host a golf tournament to raise money for scholarships in Terry and Tiff's memory. The money would go to students who wanted to go to the University of Miami, since all three of my children had a connection there. Tracey had graduated from there, Tiff was going to go there and Terry was always a huge fan of U of M. I'm sure, in part, that planning the golf tournament was Mike's way of keeping busy, while doing something wonderful that honored Terry and Tiffany. And the tournament was a huge success.

I must also tell you about Tiffany's art teacher from high school. Her name is Carla Stiles and she has sent me a memento for 25 years on Tiffany's birthday, letting me know that she has not forgotten our Tiffy. And to let me know what a wonderful mark Tiff left on her heart. How great is that? I am always in awe that I am the mother of three such awesome human beings.

Terry's friends from the Army and other friends also let me know what a special person Terry was, and what an impact he had on their lives. I always think of the piece by Thomas Campbell that says, "To live in the hearts we leave behind, is not to die."

CHAPTER 12

Where Are You God?

While I was in the depths of despair, I began to really question the why's of my life. Why me? Why again? Why, why, why. And I can't say that all the answers I begged for came rushing to me instantly. But my search to get some answers did begin in full force at that time.

I went to every denomination of church and synagogue that I could find in the area. And I would sit in the back and listen to the preacher or rabbi. But all I could hear was blah, blah, blah. I read many books that tried to explain why bad things happen to good people, or how everything happens for a reason, or how this too shall pass. But nothing felt like it applied to me and the pain that I was feeling. I know now that I just wasn't ready to accept the facts of 'what is'. And I guess I was mad that my loves were taken from me. So no amount of soothing words of explanation were being heard by me at that time.

I kept on going like the books said you should, and I waited for some magical epiphany that would let me grasp 'why', and would somehow lift the million pound weight off of my heart.

Some may think that I don't believe in God because of the spiritual beliefs that I have. But that isn't the whole truth. Religion never did 'sit well' with me, and my spiritual side always seemed to be calling out to me. And that's why I consider myself a spiritual 'being' more than a 'religious person'. So if religion wasn't helping me, I decided that I had to find my answers through spiritual ways.

And if I was mad at God and I was blaming Him for everything that was happening, then I had to find a way to figure out what in the hell I had done to make Him so mad at me. But the more I searched and read and listened to other spiritual teachers, I began to understand that all that had happened to us was not personal.

When I started thinking this way, it made more sense to me that the God that religion was speaking about didn't compute with me. I just couldn't believe the way many portrayed God to be; as an old man with a white beard who sits up on a cloud judging everyone. A God who decides which one of us lives an everlasting and glorious life, or which of us lives a terrible life and is sent to a fiery pit because we displeased Him. A God like that isn't a forgiving God, and it just didn't resonate with me because everything that I had thought about God before, made me sense that He was all about love, and all-forgiving. Operative word here being ALL. So, I just couldn't accept that He would be anything BUT Love, or anything BUT all-forgiving. So, I wasn't being punished after all. I also don't see God as having a gender. I see God as LOVE ENERGY.

I don't believe that God is making decisions for us either. Because I believe that God always keeps His promise of Free Will. I feel that God is always there with us, i.e. omnipresent, through whatever we go through that results from the decisions that WE make. I also believe that we are always being guided for our best outcomes by God/Higher Source/Divine Intelligence, or whatever you feel comfortable calling this Love Energy. I call this The All That Is. We just don't always listen to those whispers of guidance.

A very small example of this concept is that I was the 'Movie Critic' on my high school paper. That whisper was maybe telling me that if I had pursued writing for my career choice, instead of the safer choice that my mother had advised of becoming a hairdresser - - then I may have become a famous author. And this wouldn't be my first book......it could have been my 50th or 60th. WOW, I could have been another Sue Grafton for crying out loud. And I am crying out loud right now just thinking about it. LOL

From all the reading and soul-searching that I have done, it just doesn't add up for me that God is 'behind the curtain', like the Wizard of Oz, making terrible things happen. I believe that earthquakes happen because of scientific reasons. Just as hurricanes, tornadoes, and tsunamis do. These things aren't happening to punish us. They just happen. And sometimes I feel that bad things may even happen to force us to grow and expand our soul's understanding. Not that we would ever choose these horrific things with our human, physical mind.

But religion would say that God is angry and this is our punishment. And people are inclined to believe that because of reading the stories in the Bible like Sodom and Gomorrah, and the flood, and making people speak in tongues because they were being punished. Those are all interesting 'stories'....but I think they are exactly that. Stories. Stories that were made up by people who couldn't explain natural disasters back in that time. And also by the people in power at that time who needed some way to keep people in line. And it turns out that fear is a great motivator and an even greater deterrent.

For example, in the Sodom and Gomorrah story, it's amazing to me that people today can still accept that two angels were sent down from God to destroy an entire city! If anyone today would claim to be angels, sent from God to destroy cities, they would be locked up. And how about Lot offering up his daughters for the angels to do with as they pleased with! Wait......Whaaaaaat?

This is who we are supposed to believe what a God of love would do? I would think that God could come up with a better, more loving way to have us learn.

Sorry folks, but you can't have it both ways. You can't have a God who loves us unconditionally and at the same time have Him/Her/Divine Intelligence decide that we aren't loved enough to be saved from such atrocities, or that we are going to be sent to condemnation and eternal punishment in hell. Speaking of Hell....What in the hell happened to the Free Will thingy????? And the unconditional Love thingy????? Huh?

I believe that we all have the Free Will that we've all read about in the Bible – and that God, The All That Is, Divine Intelligence, allows us to make choices precisely because of the promise of Free Will.

And some of our choices may cause us to make decisions that end up with us being in an accident. Or some of our choices cause us to eat the wrong way and not exercise as we should and we eventually have a heart attack. Or some of our choices cause disease (dis-ease) because what is bothering us, eats away at our originally balanced and perfect bodies, with some sort of cancer.

I know now that I shouldn't have asked 'why me'....I should have asked 'why not me'. If God loves us all the same, as I do believe is the case, then there can be no picking and choosing, or interference by the Divine.

WE pick and choose what happens in our lives with each decision we make, i.e. Free Will. My late husband, and later my daughter and son's deaths were the result of car accidents. Not because God wanted Shirley to have the most horrific days imaginable.

Just as the movie 'The Shack' so profoundly illustrated: we parents could never be expected to choose which of our children will be doomed by our own hand and which will be allowed to sit by us for eternity because of something that they chose to do, or how they believed. Think about that for a while. Let it sink in, and if you're honest with yourself, I think you'll see it from a different perspective.

I feel that Source is an energy of pure LOVE, and that Love doesn't make any distinctions about which of [us] goes through life swimmingly, or which of [us] has an accident, or has a heart attack, or gets cancer, or.........fill in the blank.

This is also why I say that every decision and every thought that we have, leads us in a direction that will affect the unfolding of the next part of our lives. And then there's Karma.

About Karma. I don't think of Karma in the way that I used to think of it - as some 'get you' form of punishment. The way I now understand Karma is that it's really just a balancing of the Universe. It's always allowing, make that demanding balance, by bringing the same energy to us that we put out into the Universe.

When we do something loving, more loving energy comes back to us. And on the flip side, when we send out negative energy, we receive negative experiences back to us. It's all to balance the Universe. Anything less than this balancing act would throw everything in the Universe out of kilter. And that just ain't gonna happen Peeps.

Just remember that nothing little ol' you or me could ever do, or think, or believe, will change how the Universe operates. I know some people think they are the center of the Universe – but they are in for a big surprise when they find out that just isn't the case. And I sure wish I could be there to see the looks on some of their faces when they do find this out. Maybe I just will be. Ha!

Another thing to remember is that Divine Source Energy (God) IS LOVE and only sends out LOVE. So if you are demonstrating or feeling anything that is less than Love, you will feel uncomfortable. This is because feelings of negativity and hate are the ABSENCE of this Love Energy, and it means that we are going away from what Divine Energy Source IS. And what we are meant to be too.

The Universe doesn't make mistakes and is always unbiased. No favoritism at all is ever involved in balancing the WHOLE WORLD! And that's why nature is always the same. If you plant a tomato seed, you never reap a banana from what you've sown. And that goes for everything in life. Sow hate? Yup, that's what you're gonna' reap. PERIOD. That's is just the way the cookie crumbles Peeps!

Oh, we may see things that seem to be unfair or observe people who we think are doing things that they are 'getting away with'. But I promise you….everything does balance out eventually. We just have to have patience, of which we humans seem to possess very little of.

And we never do know exactly what is going on in someone else's life anyway. They may look as if they have it all, but they may be struggling in another area of their lives. They may have lots of wealth, but they are ill. They may live in a big house, but it isn't a loving Home. So, never assume and try not to judge. That isn't our job anyway. Believe me, the Universe has got this!!

And I will continue to believe the way I do until something comes along that resonates more with me. But for me to believe something, I have to feel that it's real. And the stories that I had been told as a child in those church pews just don't add up for me. But I will always respect those who do believe in those stories. It's not my place to make anyone believe the way I do.

Being a student of wanting to learn all there is to learn, I will continue to put the pieces together until I have the complete puzzle. So if I'm still around, I'll let you all know what I discovered, and share what has been shown to me. Pinky Promise! But if I have to wait until I transition to learn it all....we'll talk on the 'other side'. *wink-wink* And won't that be a hoot?!

CHAPTER 13

The Cracks Are Where the Light of Awareness Gets In

In 2008 I became completely involved, OK obsessed, about learning all that I could about The All That Is. You may call it woo-woo, but I call it my 'fully waking up' period. And the astonishing thing is that I was 60 years old at that time. And when that first glimpse of awareness did 'seep in' through the cracks, I knew that I could never turn back. Nor did I want to. You see, once you have that flash of 'knowing' that you're onto something that feels true…..you become more eager than ever to understand it even more.

I had been searching and wanting to understand where all of [us] came from…and why for years. For forever actually. What was the purpose of life? The 'story' about humans beginning in the Garden of Eden had never rung true for me. The dots never seemed to connect up squarely for me. I have since come to understand that the story of Adam and Eve was a story of symbolisms and metaphors about good and evil. And of choosing the path of fear or of wisdom. But people took it literally and the story perpetuated.

For example, A Course in Miracles explains the meaning of original sin as: "Sin is defined as lack of love. Since love is all there is, sin in the sight of the Holy Spirit is a mistake to be corrected, rather than an evil to be punished. Our sense of inadequacy, weakness, and incompletion comes from the strong investment in the scarcity principle that governs the whole world of illusions. From that point of view, we seek in others what we feel is wanting in ourselves. We love another in order to get something ourselves. That, in fact, is what passes for love in the dream world. There can be no greater mistake than that, for love is incapable of asking for anything". WOW right?

While we were living in Tennessee, I had read a book called A New Earth by Eckhart Tolle. I had always been a fan of the Oprah Winfrey TV show, so when I heard that she was going to offer a webcast with Eckhart about his book, I was very anxious to watch it.

The book was way over my level of understanding at the time that I first read it, but I still wanted to have a better understanding of what Eckhart was pointing to. So, since the house where we lived didn't have great signal reception, I would drive up to our Pro Shop at night and watch it there on the computer. I watched, took notes, and tried to absorb everything that Eckhart was saying.

I have to say that it does take a while to fully understand everything and it doesn't come all at once. But since that time, I have read and listened to many other respected and popular authors on the subject, and even some scientists, and I feel that I am now at a place where the pieces of the puzzle fit more easily into place.

There are still some pieces that I need to fill in for the whole puzzle to be complete, but I am sure that they will come.....when I am ready. And I feel now that these accounts of The All That Is, resonate with me much more than the stories about our beginnings that I had been told for so long.

Since then I have been noticing everything about everything. Of course, each day is about learning more and more because I pay closer attention now. And I also pay attention to how everyone else acts and also how I act and react as well. This habit can lead to true growth in all of us. That is if we are honest with ourselves. That's the tricky part.

Another astonishing thought that I had was, 'How did I go so many years and not even question what The All That Is – was?' The answer that came to me is that we all awaken when we are ready.

Previously, I had been allowing life to live me instead of living my life with the awareness that I was not all the labels that I had attached to myself for so many years; daughter, mother, wife, friend, hairdresser, etc.

I suddenly understood that I was not all the thoughts and labels about who I thought I was. I was the observer of all of these thoughts. The beginning of Spirituality is when we first separate who we say that we are from who we are not. What is left is who we really and truly are. Pure awareness…that is consciousness.

Knowing that we are not the thoughts that we think, but the observer of our thoughts is the most freeing thing that we can do for our awareness.

Just as we can think of a red car, and then let that thought go. Or think of a blue balloon, and then let that thought go - - we can also let thoughts go that no longer serve us. Thoughts like; they don't like me, or I'm fat, or I'm not good enough……can all be let go too. They are thoughts just like the blue balloon or the red car. This culling of our thoughts is what eventually leads us to peace of mind. "The peace that surpasses all understanding".

I have figured out that we are all [here] to understand all the parts of ourselves. Not masking who we are to the outside world. We know who we are at our core, and if we are not living an authentic life, we won't feel genuine. And that makes us uneasy. If we aren't authentic, we are always fearful that we will be 'found out'. So take the mask off and feel free!!! And if you don't like things about how you are acting, then change the way you are acting.

The way I understand it is that everything – EVERYTHING - is energy, and energy cannot be destroyed. It can only be transformed. When I fully understood this, it brought me the peace and serenity that I was looking for about losing my own loved ones. I could understand that they were not 'gone'. They just are not here in the physical or visible to MY eyes any longer. And it also allowed me to feel that I wasn't crazy when I felt that I could sense their presence.

My acceptance and understanding that our souls could visit us once we transition from our earthly bodies came from experiences I had where I just knew Terry and Tiffany were right there with me.

Like each time I am at the beach, one bird will inch up close to me and just look at me. My Tiffany was always very interested and fascinated by birds, and when that one bird comes inching up to me now, I know it's Tiff.

Does that mean I think Tiff is a bird now? No. It means that Tiffany knows that I know how she was about birds and that I would feel comfortable connecting the bird coming close to me as a way for me to know it was her spirit visiting me. And I could use the bird metaphor more easily because we humans aren't fully ready to 'see' or accept our loved ones in whatever form they may be in now.

And another time I felt the spirit of my loved ones was a time I was feeling sad and missing my son and a song came on the radio of my car. It was one of Terry's favorites. I truly believe our loved ones come to us at times that we are sad and missing them. And also when we are remembering them while are enjoying something that we used to do with them too. So, I spoke out loud and told Terry that I loved him and that I miss him and if he could just let me know that he knows this, to please give me some sort of a sign.

My son loved to ride his motorcycle and he used to do wheelies that scared me to pieces watching him do them. As soon as the words were out of my mouth about asking for a sign, a guy on a motorcycle came whizzing between my car and the car next to me - - and he did a WHEELIE! I don't care what anyone else thinks, I know it was the sign that I'd asked for. I thanked Terry and sent him my love. And I have to admit that I did shed a few more tears as I drove on.

Another time that I know Terry and Tiffany's spirits visited me was when I was driving to work not too long ago and thinking of them. I had some questions that I needed help with and I spoke out loud to them and asked for a sign that they could hear me.

As I asked my question, a bird flew next to my car. Now, I know there are birds everywhere, but this bird flew right beside my car – ON BUSY I-95 – during the morning rush hour. This lone bird was not in a flock, nor could I see another bird anywhere around. And it hovered right next to the window of my car and flew alongside of me for a while, and then flew off. I immediately teared up and said, "Hello Sweet Tiffy."

Then I thought that this must be my sign, but if a motorcycle were to come along right now, it would be my Terry telling me that he was with me as well. And yep a bright red crotch rocket (the kind that Terry used to ride) came whizzing by me in the HOV lane. I laughed because that is something that Terry would have done too. Using the lane that was specifically for 2 or more passengers as if it were his own highway. He was a rebel at times for sure.

I said hello my love to Terry too and then I thought that must be all of my sign. But no! Just then a song came on the radio and the lyrics were, "This is not a coincidence and far more than a lucky chance." It sounded like Stevie Wonder to me and I have always love Stevie, but I didn't recognize this song at all. The song didn't even play out for the whole song to finish. So, I listened intently to hear the words so I could look it up when I got home.

The name of the song was Ribbon In The Sky. How awesome, right?

I have to tread lightly here because many will say that it's ridiculous to think that we would ever 'choose' to die. I realize that our human-conditioned mind doesn't comprehend how we could ever choose death over life. But I have come to a place where I am able to accept that maybe we all do make the decision of when we will transition. Maybe we do choose when to 'leave' and when to 'drop into' our current meat suits. And which lessons we choose to learn while we have each life experience. These are our Soul Contracts.

Humor me for a moment. Let's say that we can picture in our mind while we are 'waiting on a cloud somewhere up above' – or wherever it is that we wait in between life experiences – and we have the ability to see different situations and life experiences to explore and to choose from. Say in our last life we lived as a Royal of some kind and now we want to experience what it may be like to be someone without any riches. Maybe to even be homeless or be someone who has to work very hard to make a living. With our human mind, we can't imagine ever wanting to suffer or be homeless. But our soul may want or need the experience to learn and expand our understanding and compassion.

I feel that we do choose the life that we will live. One that best teaches us lessons that will expand, grow and enrich our soul. We may even choose a life that wouldn't make any sense in our 'now life'. I understand that our 'now minds' find it hard to comprehend choosing a life that is without the creature comforts we are used to. But if we knew, on another level, that we were choosing the experience of a certain life to enhance our soul's growth, I believe that it could be better received as a possible concept.

And also, if we did somehow have the ability to know that it is just for this one 'life period', and since time is not of any essence, we may see our way to understanding how we could choose a less than optimum life experience. And always remember that our soul doesn't know anything about the concept of time, except that it only exists for our human thinking minds.

It would also be easier to accept if we would know that it wasn't a 'forever' permanent choice. Sort of like when we choose which Avatar we are going to play in a video game. Or how an actor chooses to be the 'bad guy' in a film, just to change it up a bit. Not everyone chooses to be the 'good guy' all the time because after all, it IS just a game or a movie, right? *wink-wink*

And if you were to believe that we do live for eternity, it makes sense not to get all freaked out about 'dying', because our soul would know that we will get to have another go round again, and that could take the sting out of it. Well, sort of!

I think the reason that we don't remember the contract our soul made is because knowing why we chose the life we did, would have less of an impact on how we did live it out. Or it may influence each life choice that we make along the way. It would be like knowing the end of the story before it happened. And no one likes spoilers! Well, mostly no one.

We would also have to have 'soul amnesia' for the length of time in each of our life experiences - so that we fully comprehend and completely learn the lessons of the life that we did choose.

I can see where we may not want to wake up from our 'dream life' though if we did choose a really good feeling life experience. Much like when we wake from a wonderful dream and we hurriedly try to go back to sleep to get back into the place where we left off.

And at the end of our human life, we all transform from this human experience back into our spirit soul. I do think about those 'life flashing before our eyes' stories that we've all heard about from those who have had NDE (near deaths experiences). It makes me want to be sure that I will enjoy my flashing life when my time comes.

But we do leave behind everything that we thought was so important while we were alive. And we leave those whom we love too. Whether we are wealthy or middle class or poor - everything and everyone is left behind. As the Italian Proverb says, "After the game, the king and the pawn go back into the same box".

I realize that this may not be what many Bible study groups teach us. But there are many hints in the Bible that do point to some of what I have offered here.

I have read the Bible and I've come to the conclusion that it was written so long ago that the interpretations may have been embellished or biased by the different people who interpreted it. They were taught by their parents and their parents before them. And by hearsay from people who were told the stories that were handed down from generation to generation too. These perceptions and even the translations had very different meanings back then.

And with each transmittal of the 'story', the interpretation changed a bit with each translation. This is because of the viewpoint and perceptions of each storyteller. But we do eventually end up believing what our parents taught us when we were children, most of the time. As the Jesuits maxim says, "Give me a child for the first seven years and I'll give you the man".

Google tells us, "The texts were mainly written in Biblical Hebrew, with some portions (notably in Daniel and Ezra) in Biblical Aramaic. Biblical Hebrew, sometimes called Classical Hebrew, is an archaic form of the Hebrew language. The very first translation of the Hebrew Bible was into Greek."

Play the childhood game of 'Telephone', where you sit in a circle and one person whispers something to the person next to them and that person whispers to the person next to them and it goes all the way around the circle until it gets to the last person before the first person who whispered it, and you will see that the story has changed quite a bit, or completely in translation from the first utterance to the last.

This is because we humans tend to tell it like we see it from our own perspective rather than how it really may be. We are all biased to some degree. Some more than others. So it is understandable how the Bible could have been interpreted differently than what actually transpired in 'the beginning'.

This is also true in life, when people would rather believe stories told to them of how an incident happened between two people, instead of believing what they really do know about the character of the two people involved in a scenario. They deny what they know, to protect their choice of staying blind to the facts.

These unwitting truth-benders can even include God-fearing, church-goers who sit in their pews each week, listening about non-judgment and then go outside and judge others. And some don't even wait until they do get outside! The pious do have the sharpest teeth you know!

I also accept that there are many good tenets in the Bible that teach us how we should all get along and love one another. But I can also see how some of the teachings were meant to scare people to keep them in line. We humans tend to get a bit barbaric without any laws, guidelines, or fear of repercussions if we are left to our own devices. Think 'Lord of the Flies' here.

But I will say that if the only reason that we are behaving morally is because we think someone is watching us from somewhere up above, and we are only 'good' because we are 'God-fearing' people – it really says a lot about us. Good character is doing the right thing, even when no one is watching. That's what a really good person is - in my opinion anyway.

Speaking of how we act when no one is looking. I have also known many Street Angels and House Devils in my day. House Devils are the people who behave like angelic shining examples of citizenship when they are out and about, and act like A-Holes at home. You really wouldn't recognize these people if you were to catch them off guard when they didn't think anyone was watching their behavior.

As I look back at the House Devils I have known, I recognize a common thread among them. They have a visceral need to be seen as important. And what that really means is that they don't feel very good about themselves at all. So they have to try to feel superior by making other people feel bad. And this behavior tends to be with their family members or people below their own pay grade, who they have power over. They are not the nice people they portray themselves to be in public......at all.

But since I do believe that we are all made from the energy of God/Divine Source, then I must also accept that we are all parts of THE ONE – personified. The good AND the bad. If God/The All That Is/Divine Source is omnipresent, omnipotent and omniscient - then ALL aspects of us are parts of the Divine as well. It can be no other way.

You may ask why would Source 'allow' us to come into being, and then suffer, or have fun, or otherwise live the lives that we live? The only answer that makes any sense to me is that Source is much like us. We watch movies on a screen to be entertained, knowing full well that it isn't real. We read books to satisfy a yearning to learn about something, or to be engrossed and engaged in the storyline for a time. We have children that we love to watch grow and we learn through their life experiences and choices. In that way, I feel that Divine Source gets to know Itself through our lives as well.

We are taught our beliefs, but we might ask then why do we gravitate to certain likes, such as careers, places to live and the people we choose to spend our lives with. I think this is so that we may 'discover' what makes us feel good. And then we are in the right frequency to bring even more of those good vibrations to us. The real purpose of life is to be in constant JOY! We just fudge it up with our negative thoughts most times.

Call me cray cray – or woo-woo if you like, but this understanding works for me. And I feel that if we treat others the way we wish to be treated, things do work out much better for us. Hey! I think I heard or read that somewhere? Does 'Do Unto Others' ring a bell? Hmmmmm. And I think that the time we have during our own life experience(s) can be wonderful or miserable, precisely because of the choices we make every day.

Then how exactly does that square with our having a Soul Contract? If it's all planned out before we come into this lifetime, then what does it matter what we do? Well, I'll tell you. I sense that we are always being guided by Loving Energy that adores us and only wants us to find our way 'home', with our souls having grown through the experiences of our life choices. Sound familiar parents? Don't we parents want the same with our children?

Because of this soul contract, we are allowed to learn the lessons we agreed upon before we dropped into our meat suits. However, we are able to change directions at any time during any of our 'life drop-ins' because of what I keep referring to as Free Will!

And because of these detours that we may decide to take, we may not learn what we agreed to on this go around. But no worries....we will keep coming back until we do learn them. Remember I said that 'time' is not a consideration in these decisions? If we learn the lessons as we agreed upon, great. But if we change directions, we will still have those lessons to learn as we come back again and again, until we have completed the contract we made for the growth of our soul. Eternity is never ending, right? The Bible refers to this as everlasting and eternity.

In the Gnostic Gospel of Thomas Jesus said, "If you bring forth what is within you, what you bring forth will save you. If you do not bring forth what is within you....what you do not bring forth will destroy you." But only for this lifetime. There's always a next one so we can tidy up those pesky unfinished, unlearned lessons.

Try to live your life in Hi-Def my friends.....not in black and white. And start by being honest with yourself about what and why the people and situations are arising in your life. This is your life Peeps... not a dress rehearsal...so make it worth the time we are given to experience this precious gift.

And as Abraham says, you can't get it wrong and you never get it done. We are ever expanding awareness, so if we are done, then we really and truly are done! Finito.

Some of us may have wanted to learn the lesson of trust, so we are given many situations that include trust in our lessons. Until we have learned the lesson of trust that we wanted to learn, there will be a pattern that keeps showing up for us that includes the concept of trust in our life, until we resolve and learn that lesson.

Maybe some of us may have wanted to learn the lessons of Forgiveness. Therefore, our life will give us many situations to either forgive others or to ask for forgiveness for ourselves.

Always keep in mind that any negative energy that 'needs' to be dispelled, will keep coming back to us to be resolved. So when you can name where the negative energy came from, remember to bless it and wish it well so that it can leave of your Storyboard.

And if we don't resolve or learn a particular lesson in this lifetime, then as I mentioned earlier – We'll be baaaaaaaack. So no worries, you'll get a chance to learn it in one lifetime....or another.

I have had many sage teachers along the way in my search for answers about The All That Is, and some of the concepts offered felt right. Other times, what was offered didn't feel so right. So I would take the path that did feel right to me, because I truly believe that Higher Source is always guiding us for what is best for each of us, on our own path. And we can sense which is right if we listen to our gut (intuition).

This is why we change how we believe at times. I honestly try to keep an open mind when I am searching. If I insist only on believing what I already think I know – then I will never expand my awareness. And expanding our awareness is what we are all supposed to do as we find our way back 'home'.

Having a closed mind is actually debilitating. It keeps you stuck in places that may not be serving you well any longer. I know it's scary to change what we have been told to believe all of our life. But the more we can understand that just like there are many varieties of flowers, and that no two snowflakes are alike – we humans are all different too. One is not better than the next, just uniquely and beautifully different. And those who have minds that are mostly closed shut….are the very ones who make fun of those whose minds are open and willing to understand.

The thing that always amazes me is that when we are digging a big old hairy hole in our life that we don't like, why we just don't stop digging? What I mean is that it appears that some people hear the whispers of guidance from Source and do something about it, while others need a brick to hit them on the head. Some get 'wake-up calls' and just hit the snooze button over and over again. And some just leave this earthly plane never having 'gotten it' at all. But then I think that this IS part of their own unique path of learning.

I know people who blame their past on the problems they currently have in their lives. But there is an expiration date for blaming everyone else for our problems. There is a time when you have to pull up your big girl or big boy panties and deal with whatever there is to deal with in your life. There is a limit on how long you should stay at whatever place it was that you seem to be stuck. And this process starts with awareness. However, since awareness only comes to us when we are ready….. then there's also THAT!

I believe that we all have spiritual guides and these guides only want to help us find our best possible way. It's like the 'you're getting hot, no you're getting cold' game that we played as kids. These guides are always letting us know if we are getting closer to, or farther away from understanding what we came here to understand. It's that feeling we get in our gut that is trying to warn us that we are in danger, or that we are veering off on the wrong path. Or on the flip side, that it feels like Goldilocks's kind of 'juu-uust right'.

My instincts give me signs when I experience other things too. For example, I have always loved Victorian homes, and that period of history. The first time I went to New England, I felt as if I were home. As if I had lived there once upon a time. I can't come up with any other explanation as to why I gravitate to that area except that maybe I had lived there in another life. Just ask yourself if you have ever had a similar feeling about someplace you visited for the very first time. And just what does make us we feel an inclination to one place over another?

I feel this goes for people we meet as well. We can meet some people and feel like we've known them a hundred years. Maybe we have? We just click and feel so comfortable with them. More so than with some people that we've known most of our lives. And even more than some family. Hmmmmmmmmm. Just sayin'.

I have come to trust that the You-niverse always has my back – even when I'm being a dumb-ass. And if we take the time to listen to how we are feeling, the Universe will always point us in the right direction for us to get back on course.

Trust is the one thing that we have to muster up when it seems as if our whole life is in the dumps. And we have to trust that each lesson we are experiencing, whether wonderful or crappy as hell, is what we have asked for to learn the lesson that lies within.

CHAPTER 14

Playing the Game With The All That Is

This 'game of life' sure does play with us some days. And it doesn't always feel so much like a game. But if we learn 'how' the game is played.....it can be much more enjoyable.

First, we must know that there are rules of the game. Like, our thoughts become things, so flip any negative thoughts you may be having to pleasant ones as soon as you notice you are having negative thoughts.

Another thing I've read is that the Universe never hears 'No' - and brings to us what we think about most. So even if you are thinking or saying that you don't want XYZ on your path – the Universe hears XYZ, and it appears on your path. It can be tricky when we are going through crap storms to remember that all we have to do to alter a current life experience is to change our thoughts to what we WOULD like and stop focusing on what we DON'T want. I say 'all we have to do' as if it's easy to do. But it really takes focus and practice.

Acceptance is also a biggy. Many think that if we accept XYZ, then we are saying we want or like whatever XYZ is appearing in our lives. But what it actually means is that once an unwelcome XYZ has shown up for you, you must acknowledge it and then you can change course directions. There is no sense in trying to pretend that XYZ hasn't surfaced on your life path. Just look at it, try to figure out why it appeared, learn the lesson from it – and move the hell away from it and onto a brighter, happier experience. As I've been known to say a time or two – "just try not to get any on you"!

So many people say that they want to be happy, but when something negative turns up in their life.....they get angry or crabby or upset. Oh, I get it! You only want to be happy until and unless XYZ happens? Uh Uh, oh no you di-ent! That's conditional happiness, not true happiness. Get it?

As the wise sages say – "Thoughts become things" and "What we resist, persists".

I have found that life is a series of situations that involve choosing to either react or respond.

Hopefully, somewhere along the line, we learn that responding is far better than reacting. Responding involves thinking. Reacting is a pattern that usually involves someone pushing our buttons. When we react, we give away our power. When we take the time to think and then respond, we retain our power.

I even find myself at times having a knee-jerk reflex to argue back when I am reading posts on Facebook sometimes from people who have no earthly clue what they are speaking about. They remind me of the Mark Twain quote: "It's better to remain silent and be thought a fool than to speak and to remove all doubt."

So then I just scroll on by because nothing I could say or add will change the opinion of someone who is so close-minded that they cannot see or hear anything except what they want to see or hear.

Take the time to think before lashing back when someone is spewing vitriol. It will make for a much more peaceful state of mind. For you, not them. Let them spew. Maybe no one ever listens to them in their lives, and Social Media is all they have to amuse themselves with.

Another tricky coping skill of life's game is about caring. Of course, we care about our family, and about saving our environment, having good health and all the important things in life. But when we can get to the place in our lives that we no longer care 'about' what others think of us, and we don't allow their feelings to cloud and color our own thoughts and feelings about our own selves, then we are closer to becoming who we are supposed to be. It goes without saying – but I'll say it anyway – if we live our lives with honor and good character, then whatever anyone says about us that is negative will not bother us at all. If someone judges you by the opinion of someone else, then they aren't using their own beanie. And that can be a very dangerous thing for sure! And I just say, shame on them.

The thing about character is that it can take a lifetime to earn respect for your character, and only one wrong decision to lose it. And a good reputation is something that is much harder to get back once you lose it. It's not so much about the opinion of others that matters– but our own opinion of ourselves that should mean the most to us. We do have to look in the mirror each day.

Do we make foolish decisions in life? You betcha'. But if we do make mistakes that are not of a malicious nature, then there will be less of a blotch on our character than if we did make decisions that were meant to harm. It's really a pretty easy concept to understand. Make a mistake – learn and grow from it. Do mean things – just sit back and wait for the balance of Karma to whack you on the noggin'. PERIOD.

I sometimes think that if I had made better choices in life that I would be in a different place than I am now. Not that I have it bad mind you, but I could have made better choices so that I wouldn't have a smidgen of financial worries in my later years.

But then I see-saw back and think that if I hadn't had all the experiences that I've had, I may not be the 'me' that I am today. And to tell the truth, I'm pretty OK with who I have evolved into. (She says humbly...lol)

We would never have owned a restaurant and met so many of our customers that became such good friends. Like our forever friend Richard, and also Wayne and Gail Batten, and Maria and Clyde Grampa, and many others who we also met during our time at our restaurant.

We would never have owned a golf course and re-built it from the ground up (literally) and met so many wonderful people there as well. Many who have remained treasured friends ever since. I can't imagine our life without friends like the Hopper's, the Forbess's, Betty Baker and so many more dear friends that we made while at the golf course. And so many of our members went far and beyond to help us while we were there.

So, were they really failures? You would have to define failure and success to actually find that answer. I feel a great accomplishment in having had those experiences. Even if they had turned out differently and we had become bazillionaires from either of them. We gained so many wonderful friendships that we would never have had, had we not undertaken those ventures.

Maybe total or lasting success wasn't what was supposed to happen for my soul's journey. Maybe I was supposed to feel pride in those great accomplishments, only for them to take a different turn and then teach me humility – without anger or blame. And I can accept that.

Heck, our 45th president of the USA had many bankruptcies and still managed to become the leader of the free world, so why should we feel bad about how some of our business attempts turned out? There were still many blessings intermingled in all of our endeavors.

And maybe the best lesson I took away from any 'failure' I may have had is that it's not as important what you accomplished, as who are after all is said and done. If you can remain true to yourself in all things, I would call that being successful AF.

Then there are those people who have literally come up from nothing and for some odd reason, they appear to have forgotten where they did come from, and who helped them get where they are today. They now appear to look down on those who have less – when they themselves had much less at one time too.

I feel that if you are truly a good person, you will treat the janitor the same as the CEO. After all, Janitor and CEO are just labels. The person is the real thing. And feelings are more important than labels. To those who value the dollar more than a person, I offer the quote by Patrick Meagher, "Some people are so poor that all they have is their money".

I have had a lot of financial stability in my life and I have had times of having much less. What I found in each of these life experiences is that I'm still 'me' – with or without all the stuff and the money. And as I like to say – you can't take it with you anyway, and the proof is that you never see a U-Haul behind a hearse.

The times in my life that I had a lot of 'stuff and things' were great times. But the times that the stuff, things, and money were lean, weren't all that bad either. At one time, no one could have made me think that I could live without all my 'stuff'. But time and circumstances proved that I had to downsize and give up a lot of my 'stuff'.

The funny thing about it is that the more stuff that I got rid of…….the more freeing it felt. There was less to worry about. Less to try to figure out where to store the stuff. Less to keep clean. It was definitely a life lesson in the making. As is everything.

When we moved back to Florida from Tennessee, we had downsized more than I ever would have imagined that I could. But we still had more stuff than would fit in our little apartment that my hubby had found for us by the ocean. So Mike said we could get a storage unit to fit our 'stuff' in until we got a bigger apartment. Okie Dokie Artichokie! Done and done.

We did eventually move into another apartment a few years later. This one was on the Intracoastal Waterway (ICW) in Fort Lauderdale. The views were magnificent – but the apartment was still too small to fit all of our stored stuff into.

Then we moved to a bigger apartment in Lauderhill. Yeah, we tend to move a lot. Do I love moving? Hell no! Who does? But I digress. The larger apartment in Lauderhill was very large – BUT, it was furnished. Sooooooo, there was no room for our own stuff again.

Then we moved again. Do you see a pattern here? I do and I guess it's one of those lessons I haven't figured out yet. But I have learned to bloom wherever I am planted and appreciate what I have instead of worrying about what I don't have. And that's not a bad way to try to live. In fact, IMHO, it's the only way. So, maybe that was my lesson: Don't get overly attached to things and learn to LET GO!

Then….we moved again to Pompano Beach. That apartment was right on the beach. RIGHT ON THE FREAKING BEACH I SAY!!! BUT….it also was furnished. Blah, Blah, Blah.

THEN….yep you guessed it – moving time again. But this time, at least it was in the same building, only 10 floors up into the Penthouse on the 20th story. It was only called the penthouse because it was on the top floor, not because we were rich folk.

There were 9 other apartments on the penthouse floor, so it wasn't what you usually think of when you hear 'penthouse'. But it sure felt like a penthouse to us….and we had the same views as the millionaires who own their magnificent homes on the ocean. And we sure did love it there. I could peer out and see the ocean right from our kitchen sink. It sure made doing the dishes a whole lot more enjoyable!

We happily stayed in that Pompano Beach condo for 4 years. Ahhh-hhhh, 4 lovely years without packing boxes and moving to a different location. All I had to do with this move up to the 20th floor was fill the shopping cart that the condo provided for bringing your groceries up to your apartment, and unload our stuff. I'd fill the cart with our belongings, one trip at a time, and get on the elevator and move our stuff into the new unit. Much, much easier than boxing everything up and trucking it somewhere else. Don't get me wrong, it was still moving – but a lot less 'moving agony'.

The back of the apartment was on the ocean, with a full and glorious view of the Atlantic Ocean. We could enjoy the magnificent sunrises each day from our kitchen and living room windows. The Intracoastal Waterway (ICW) was viewable from the front of the building and treated us with stunning evening sunsets. My daughter lives on the other side of the ICW and we could walk to each other's houses. We were living large.

The little grands always loved to come to Gommy and Gpa Mike's 'hotel house' on the beach. The pool was enormous and the beach was right beyond the pool. And we were very, very grateful. ALWAYS!

But back to the penthouse apartment and the eventual debacle that lay in wait for us. Of which we were completely unaware. What had happened is that the unit had been owned by a man who died and he had left owing a lot of back HOA dues, fees, and unpaid property taxes. After a while, the lawyers for the condo claimed the unit for the past dues and fees. At least they thought they had claimed it. But nooooooo. Uh Uh. Not so fast condo board peeps!

Then there was a new person who got involved in the mix. Sometime during the unfolding saga of the gorgeous ocean view penthouse apartment, this new guy on the scene 'thought' that he bought the unit on the courthouse steps for the property taxes. That's the term for the public being able to purchase a home for property taxes owed. But noooooo. Uh Uh. Not so fast new owner guy!

Soooooo, the new 'owner', who thought he had bought the unit 'for a song', didn't get along with the condo board people very well because they all fought back and forth about the ownership of the unit, and who owed what to whom.

The new 'owner' of the unit finally got fed up and just wanted to sell it. We were given 2 weeks – in the middle of high season, in Florida I might add – to get out and find a new place. YIKES, right? But I had gotten much better at not thinking thoughts of jumping from a tall building, which we happened to be living in at the time coincidentally, when upsetting and unwanted things were thrown at me. I've finally accepted that things always do seem to work out, whether I become hysterical or not. So, not getting hysterical is therefore my better choice. And one that doesn't involve jumping. Ommmmmmmm.

Before, when Mike and I had needed to move from the 10th floor, it was because that owner died as well, and they wanted to sell that unit. UGH, right? If everyone would just stay alive, it would save us a lot of trouble having to move (she says most 'caringly').

All the while the penthouse unit drama was going on behind the scenes, Mike and I were just loving and enjoying our home with its magnificent ocean view.

Mike was nicknamed the Mayor of the Beach. He would go out each evening when he got home from work and sit on the beach and watch the stars and the moon when they came out, and smoke cigars. He knew everyone who walked by him and they knew him. Did I mention that he could talk to a rock? I am more of a keep to myself kind of person, but he is truly a people-person and he wouldn't miss many evenings of sitting on the beach and talking to the beach walkers.

I often wish I were more like Mike – but you know how it is, opposites attract. It's probably supposed to be that way so that we can learn from each other. I've certainly learned a lot from him and he's told me that I've helped him quite a bit in all of our years together too. So, Check and Check!

Mike would sit on the beach in the dark too. He kidded that it was his Zen time. He was joking with me of course because I am the 'woo-woo' in the family. He's woo-woo too, he just doesn't know it. He always expects something to happen and it does. BINGO. And DUH….. that IS the definition of woo-woo after all!

Just recently it was proven to me once again just how my woo-wooness is 'contagious', or at least it's rubbing off on my Honey Bun. What happened was one day at my work, a homeless man was sitting on a bench outside of the shop. I had watched him for a few days as he checked the garbage cans for food and walked back and forth before sitting on the bench to rest. So, I texted my husband what I had been observing and that I felt bad for the man. And do you know what my husband texted back to me? "He is there to remind us how lucky we are."

BAM! Told ya' Mike gets it! And he gets the whispers that I speak of too. I know hearing about the homeless man made my husband as sad as it did me, but he saw the message within the encounter before ol' woo-woo me did. It also reminded me of the quote by John Bradford, "There but for the grace of God go I."

I try to begin my day, every day, remembering how lucky we are and showing how grateful I am by being even more kind and considerate and respectful of others who cross my path.

Anywhooooo, back to Mike sitting on the beach. April to October is 'Turtle Nesting Time' in our part of the world. Mike would often come in and tell me he had seen a turtle lay her eggs right next to him. Some nights there would be 2 or 3 turtles lay eggs. Sure nuff…..I'd go out to the beach the next day and there would be 2 or 3 or however many nesting sites that had been added the night before. I knew this because the 'turtle people' – the people who volunteer to stake out the nests - had put orange ribbons and stakes up around the new nests, and dated them so they could tell when it was time for them to hatch. The whole nesting and hatching of turtles is quite interesting. And we were able to observe it from our own 'backyard'!

Mike had told our friend Doug about the turtles one day. He was a bit skeptical about Mike's description of how he watched the mama turtles lay their eggs on the beach each night. So, Mike invited him to come over one night and see for himself. So, he and another friend did come over. We all got in our beach chairs and sat. And waited.....

We talked and visited and enjoyed the night air, filled with the salty smell of the ocean, and enjoyed the gorgeous moon that lit up the sky and reflected on the ocean. I think they were getting even more skeptical when Mike said, "Just wait. In 30 minutes a turtle will come out and lay her eggs." They rolled their eyes. Yeah, right Mike. Wellll, remember how I told you that Mike was an 'unawares woo-woo'? Lo and behold, within 30 minutes a big turtle came very slowly out of the water and she came up right next to our friend. If I could have seen our friend's eyes, I'm quite sure that they had stopped rolling them right about then. But some guy running on the beach came by and spooked her and she went back in the water. DANG! We were bummed but our friends said they were just happy to have seen it for themselves.

Then ol' woo-woo Mike said to wait a little bit longer because he felt she was going to come back and finish her egg laying. I think I sensed more eye-rolling again.

But yep....after a bit, she did come back out of the water and dug a hole and laid her eggs in it. I told you not to mess with Mike when he has a feeling! We used to joke that when he REALLY had a feeling, he would say that he was twitching. And THAT's why they call him Smokin' Mike!

He's smokin' hot about his feelings. And he's usually right – especially when twitching is involved.

A very interesting fact about turtles is that the very same turtles come back year after year to the exact same spot to lay their eggs. And the little turtles that do survive, come back to the same spot to lay their eggs as well after they are grown. Amazing, right?

Wikipedia says, 'There are several different kinds of marine animals that demonstrate natal homing. The most commonly known is the sea turtle. Loggerhead sea turtles are thought to show two different types of homing. The first of which comes in the early stages of life. When first heading out to sea, the animals are carried out by tides and currents with little swimming involved. Recent studies now show that the animals demonstrate homing to feeding grounds near their natal birthplace. Turtles of a specific natal beach, show differences in their mitochondrial DNA haplotypes that distinguish them from turtles of other nesting areas. Many turtles from the same beaches show up at the same feeding areas.

Once reaching sexual maturity in the Atlantic Oceans, the female Loggerhead makes the long trip back to her natal beach to lay her eggs. The Loggerhead sea turtle in the North Atlantic covers more than 9,000 miles, round trip, to lay eggs on the North American shore".

You can call it mitochondrial DNA or whatever you like, but I prefer to think that we are all being 'experienced' BY Divine Source and that's why everything happens as it does. Just as birds migrate to and from the same place every year, I think [we] are all born with a journey of our choosing. And I just can't buy that everything merely happens randomly, because Nature is not random.

I believe that Divine Source has figured everything out just perfectly. It's us who interfere with perfection and screw up our lives and other people's lives too by trying to mess with Mother Nature. But I also believe that nothing is ever lost, not even in the things that we do when we do screw things up. The real machinations don't ever really change – we just have 'Life Turbulence' for a while and then the mud settles and the lotus blooms.

There are lessons in every situation, every meet up, and every experience. We just have to notice the lesson. And hear the Divine whispers.

CHAPTER 15

Not So Grimm Fairy Tales

I also think that we are given hints along the way through movies, songs, Fairy Tales and Fables that we have heard since we were children. Have you ever noticed the hidden truths, messages and meanings in Fairy Tales and childhood songs like the ones that we learned when we were young? Uh....I have. Of course I have. Ha!

Take Cinderella for example. The story really illustrates to us that we should never allow others to decide our fate. The Wizard of Oz demonstrates that all the qualities we wish to acquire like courage, kindness, and intelligence.... are qualities that we already possess.

And how about Alice in Wonderland? When Alice says, "This is impossible!" – The Mad Hatter responds, "Only if you believe it is." And the Queen advises Alice about thinking that things are impossible and says, "I daresay you haven't had much practice. When I was your age, I always did it for half-an-hour a day. Why, sometimes I've believed as many as six impossible things before breakfast".

Many other Fairy Tales uncover our inner fears and insecurities. And the song Row, Row, Row Your Boat points to life being a spiritual journey, experienced as a dream. I'm sure there are many more that I just haven't put together yet. But I'm always looking for my next A-Ha! And when I do get them, they are always knee-slappers and head smacks all in one.

I really believe that we are never too old for Fairy Tales because they allow us to hope that there is always a chance for a happily ever after. And on a deeper level – we ARE living in a 'dream world'. And it's one in which we are the dream AND the dreamer. So, kiss the frog, wear the dress, wish upon a star, outsmart the witch – and follow your own yellow brick road to believing that your dreams really can come true.

Our Divine Guidance always starts out as a whisper. Then it becomes a 'tap on the shoulder', and then if we still don't listen, there are bricks to the head! After a few of those bricks to the head, you do tend to listen for the whispers more attentively.

The gut feelings we get, and the whispers from our 'spirit-guides and teachers', and the numerical sequences we see a lot, are all pointers that are meant to nudge us in the right direction for our growth and understanding.

There are also people who enter our lives who have lessons to teach us as well. Actually, there is no one who we meet that is not meant to cross our path. Everyone is carrying a lesson for us to learn from. And we are lessons to them as well. I've learned that we possess many powers that we never knew we had.

Those who don't share my ideas about The All That Is may not agree with me, but a closed mind won't consider anything different than what it has been taught.

As I've gotten older.......there are many, many things that I've learned that have proven to me that holding fast to a certain belief was just a habit that was not serving me any longer. And I had to unlearn those things.

What if the soul had a desire to have a more understanding, compassionate, and inclusive life experience? So what showed up on that Storyboard were examples and opportunities to comprehend what it feels like to be marginalized? What it feels like to be debased? To feel scorned and judged?

It would seem as if the opposite of what we think that we want to experience as our physical selves is what comes up for us at times. But maybe that's because until we know what it's like to personally feel these opposing life situations, we won't actually 'get it'.

You see, words don't teach. Only experiencing something personally teaches us anything. It's like the analogy of your neighbor losing their home in a financial downturn. You call that a recession. If you lose your own home in the downturn, you call that a depression. Both have lost homes, but when it happens in our own life, it takes on a deeper meaning to us.

So, short story looooong, we should always try to practice compassion for those who are experiencing any downturns of any kind in their lives. And we also never know what soul contract that is being played out.

This may just be what the Scriptures meant when offering, "Judge not, lest ye be judged". We must honor each other's place on life's journey.

My grandson Brandon and I were discussing the meaning of word Namaste recently. He had the country of India as his class project and he said that Namaste was used as a greeting for hello and good-bye. I explained that it also means: "My soul honors your soul. I honor the place within you where the entire Universe resides; I honor the place within you of love, of light, of truth, of peace; I honor the place within you, where, when you are in that place in you, and I am in that place in me, we are one."

I remember when I was about 8 years old and playing with the other kids in the neighborhood, we had climbed up onto a lean-to (shed thingy). With the weight of us on the roof of it, it tore loose from the building it was attached to and fell. I was pinned underneath. The other kids started screaming and some of the moms came out of their homes and were standing around, watching in horror. Well, bad news travels fast and somehow word got to my mom that I was pinned under the roof of the shed. I remember her literally running to me and in one big heave-ho, mom lifted the shed up and I got out from under it.

My mom was very relieved that I wasn't badly hurt, but she was as mad as a Mama Bear that the other mom's hadn't tried to help me. She screamed at them, asking them why in the hell didn't they all get together and try to lift the shed roof themselves? I don't know what they said, but I was sure impressed that my mom had the power to save me.

This taught me, at a very young age, that we all possess powers that we have never tapped into and didn't even realize that we had. And much later in my life, I knew exactly what Glinda the Good Witch from the Wizard of Oz meant when she said, "You've always had the power my dear. You just had to learn it for yourself."

Some people teach us what we DON'T WANT to be like. But I have found that some of the fiercest, meanest and menacing people who have crossed my path have eventually proven to be the most notable teachers for my own spiritual growth. These poor souls just don't seem to ever get it because their ego is so big that they don't think that anyone else matters….except them and their opinion.

But then I remind myself that they chose to experience their path too. They must have wanted to know what it felt like to be obnoxious, pompous asses and be so self-centered…….OOPSIE…..I just let a little judgment seep out there. Sorry, my bad - - and so un-awakened of me!

AHEM. We do have to be very mindful of 'falling off the unicorn wagon' at times, don't ya' know? (Excuse me as I adjust my tilted halo).

Then there are those who shine a light so bright that it illuminates the path for others so that we can see better where it is that we should be heading.

Thankfully, I have had more of the light-carriers on my journey than the nasty ones. But I thank each one for the part that they played in my life. And they've all played their 'parts' exactly as they should have, for me to learn. So, BRAVO to them as well!

Unintentionally or not, we humans do mess things up from time to time. But eventually, because nothing is ever wasted, all experiences are used for our growth and the expansion of our souls. And one day, we will understand it all. Every puzzle piece has its place. We just don't always see it. It helps to remember that the You-niverse doesn't make mistakes.

As of right now, we live in Palm Beach, right across from the beach, and we've been here for a few years now. I am always just one thought away from wondering when the next 'moving shoe' will drop again and the search for our newest home will begin. Hey, maybe that's why we keep moving, right? Oy! Stop that Shirley! DUH!!

But I must admit that every place we've moved to has been another great experience and another chance to meet more people and broaden our horizons. So it hasn't been all bad! Except for the packing. Did I mention that I HATE PACKING?????? Yeah, I think I did.

CHAPTER 16

Just Let it Gooooo

In between some of our many moves, my hubby who is a lot more evolved in the letting stuff go department, said there would be no more paying for our stuff to be stored. Oh, I cried and balked and kicked at the idea of getting rid of any of my 'wonderful and I can't live without stuff'! But it didn't work. Mike said that if I could name all of the stuff in the storage unit, then I could keep it. Hmmmmm. No fair! That was not a deal that I wanted to agree to. But of course he was right. But don't tell him I said so.

So we went to the storage unit and went through all of my 'wonderful and I can't live without stuff' and I kept all of the stuff that I really and truly couldn't live without. Like pictures of my family, mementos and knick-knacks my Mom had left me, some of Terry and Tiffany's things.....stuff like that. And you know what my hubby did with all of the rest of the stuff? He gave it to the guys who worked in maintenance on the golf course where he worked. HE GAVE IT TO THEM!

Did I mention that I've figured out that my hubby is one of my life teachers who gets the lessons and concepts that I should be getting; like being generous brings much more back to you than holding on with a death grip? Yeah, I know I did. Well, this was one of the examples of him giving the 'shirt' off of MY back.

Don't worry though because I teach him the life concepts that he has a hard time with too. I like to say that there's a lid for every pot and he is my lid some days and on other days I am his lid. But what I did find out by giving all that 'stuff' away is that it felt good when my hubby told me how those maintenance workers were so excited to be picking out stuff to bring home for their families. Stuff that included some pretty nice clothes, un-worn shoes, houseware goods, huge pots and pans, and other things that they probably never would have been able to afford on their pay scale. But I did have a little chuckle when I thought that now MY stuff was THEIR stuff, and it was their problem to figure out what to do with from here on out. LOL

Another of my A-Ha's is that I've known several people who have so much guilt and shame about their life choices that it's ruining their 'now' life. I want to share with them that there is a big difference between guilt and shame. Guilt is OK. Shame is not. As long as you did what you did without malice, then it's OK to feel guilty about what you did because it may have hurt others. But that is no reason to feel ashamed. Shame means you feel badly about WHO you are. Guilt means you feel badly about WHAT you DID. They are two very different and distinct emotions.

I have done some things in my life that I feel guilty about, but I know in my heart of hearts that I didn't do anything to harm anyone else on purpose. Was I naive? Yes. Was I afraid at the time and did something un-wise because of that fear, and not thinking correctly at the time? Yes. But I don't feel ashamed of what I did because my intent was not to harm anyone. Selfish? Yes. But not with any malice. I may have just been uncon-scious (not awake) at the time as to what the collateral damage could have been. And I also feel that if we have any conscience at all, it will keep us from doing the same thing that we felt guilty about - - ever again.

I can't think of anyone who can say that they have never done anything that they don't feel guilty about. I love the proverb about people who live in glass houses shouldn't throw stones. But if you've done something to feel ashamed of – then that's a different story all together. I can't help you with that one. Sorry, but you're on your own, and it's between you and whomever you personally or spiritually answer to. And that is way higher than my pay grade.

All in all, I can say that my life feels pretty much blessed. Of course the sad and painful times were the worst anyone could ever imagine, but the sun did come out again and there were times, occasions and relationships that I would never have enjoyed, had I jumped in those holes that my 'babies' were being buried in.

My daughter Tracey married a wonderful man named Johnny and they have 2 beautiful, intelligent and perfect children (says a totally unbiased Gommy). A girl, Samantha, who is the light of my life, and a boy, Brandon, who is as well. They are as different as day and night but they complement each other to a tee with their warm hearts and love for all. It is so heart-warming to see siblings love each other so much. It reminds me of my own 3 children. And they are very kind. I feel that kindness will always pave the way to a fulfilling life. I love the sentiment that says it's better to be without gold than without family.

My son Terry's daughter, my granddaughter Megan, had a little boy named Henry a little over 2 years year ago and he made me a Great Gommy! Henry is the cutest little boy and is the light of Megan and Jeff's life. My grandson 'lil' Terry, who is now over 6 feet tall and the spittin' image of his Dad, is a wonderful man who has the heart of a giant. I know their Dad is proud of them and is always watching over them.

My hubby's son Mikey married Fio and they have 3 of the cutest little ones you could imagine. Their names are Kyra, Kylie, and Gino. They have recently moved to the Memphis area, so my hubby is bummed that he won't be seeing them as much as he would like. But the good part is that my husband is from Memphis, so he can go visit them, along with all of the great friends that we have from our days of owning the golf course in that part of the country.

The many friends we made have kept in touch all these years later. They have left an indelible and lasting place in our hearts. I can honestly say that our friends from Tennessee and Mississippi are some of the best people anyone could ever have as friends. I've found that Life has many nuggets of joy wedged in between some of the huge disappointments and sad times that we have in life. I guess that's called the Silver Lining!

I think the best thing we can ask for in life is to know that our children are happy and will be just fine without us when we are no longer here. No one wants to leave this world, but no one gets out alive either. And knowing that you brought up good people so that they can bring up good people, is a very satisfying feeling. We are very blessed in that part of our lives too. I always remember the saying that says we are only as happy as our least happy child. And boy, ain't that the truffff??

But we do have to let go of what isn't serving us any longer. It may be stuff that we let go of, or our feelings about things, or even people sometimes, and other times it's the places where we are living.

CHAPTER 17

Gommy's Going to Do Whaaaaat?

A funny story about the time we lived in Tennessee and had the golf course is that my son's son, Terry, was having a hard time in school down in Florida. He was at that hard age where he just didn't give a darn about school and he wasn't passing. His mom asked if he could come up and stay with Mike and me for a school year. Of course we said we'd love to have him stay with us.

So, up came 'little Terry', all 6 feet tall of him, and having to repeat the 9th grade. He was the stereotypical teen with a chip on his shoulder, and he sure wasn't looking forward to spending a year with Gommy and Gpa Mike under the conditions he found himself to be in.

He and Megan had spent a few weeks at a time for summer vacations with us before, and they had enjoyed it very much. But 'boot camp' with Gommy and Grandpa, and staying the whole school year was a whole 'nother' story for sure!

Of course, things were a bit different at Gommy and Gpa's when you are living with us, as opposed to just visiting. We expected Terry to share the load and help us out at the golf course after school. Terry is a smart guy and he really did help us a lot. All the members at the golf course loved him too. We paid him for working for us, but we didn't give him the money until he was going to go back home. He didn't have any expenses living with us, so this was a good way for him to save some moolah for when he went back home again! There wasn't a whole lot to spend money on in the country anyway. Even the 'picture show' at the Luez Theater in town was only $2.00 for admission. And no, that isn't a typo!

We used to go to the Sonic Drive-In in Bolivar on Tuesday's because they had a 5 Burgers for $5.00 special. Boy, did they lose out on Terry! He used to also go to the Chinese Buffet in Bolivar with some of the crew from the course. 'All you can eat' takes on a totally different meaning when you are a growing teenaged boy!

Terry's time with us started off just fine, but then the troubles began when I asked him why he didn't have any homework? He told me that he didn't have any homework. Hmmmmm, I guess he thought this was Gommy's first 'rodeo' in raising teens. Boy was he WRONG!

The next day, instead of dropping him off at the bus stop, I drove out through the entrance gate of our community. He asked me where we were going. I told him that I wanted to have a talk with the teachers and tell them that I thought it was terrible that they didn't give him homework. *wink-wink* I could sense that he was literally squirming in his seat.

When we got to school, the faculty and office staff told me a completely different story. Hmmmmm. Big surprise? No, of course I was expecting as much. So, I told Terry that even though I was very busy at the golf course, I wanted to do whatever I could for him, especially since he was my son's son. I wanted to make sure that we did what my son wasn't able to do for him and make sure that we did whatever we could do to see that he passed the 9th grade.

Each day for a week, I took Terry to school and I sat by him in EVERY CLASS THAT HE HAD. Yep, I pulled up a chair right next to him and [we] took notes. I even made out a spreadsheet so that his teachers could fill in whatever homework he had each day. You know, just in case he forgot again. (Insert Big Grin here).

School is a lot different nowadays than when we went to school, so even though Gpa Mike is a savant when it comes to Math, that isn't the way the teachers teach Math now. So, I had to Fax the Math homework to my daughter Tracey and her engineer husband John, and they helped Terry with his Math all year so that he could pass. I could help him with the other subjects, but Math is definitely not in my wheelhouse of academic expertise. It turns out that it really does 'take a village' to help children do well. And our 'village' spanned a number of states and included Terry's Aunt Tracey and Uncle John in the 'village'.

Was Terry mortified that his Grandma sat next to him in his classes each day? You betcha. Almost as much as when it was lunch time and I just hung out with him and the other kids. He assured me that it wasn't necessary, but I didn't want him to feel lonely or miss me. Bwahaha!

At first, the other kids asked who I was and before he could answer, I told them I was Terrys' Grandma and that he needed me to be with him until he got the hang of his new school and how the homework thingy worked.

Believe it or not, Terry still speaks to me today – LOL. And he's in his 20's now and is a grown and very handsome man. If I say so myself. We still have a few laughs about those times. But you know what? Terry passed that year and went on to the 10th grade with flying colors. He eventually went back to his Mom in Florida, ready for more book learnin'.

CHAPTER 18

Aging is tiresome, but it beats the alternative!

This may be a good place to explain how an older person feels about getting older. At least to me, and I do fit into that older person category now. I don't feel old on the inside. It's only when I look in the mirror or look at older pictures of myself when I was young, that I can see that I am not young anymore. Age changes our outsides, not our insides.

Now that I am in my 7th decade, I find that 'getting older' is really not for sissies. And I say this as a pretty fortunate, relatively healthy senior myself. I still don't take any medications (except for the occasional Tylenol (when my legs tell me that they want me to sit down….and there is still more of my day left).

Any time I have to change primary doctors or my health insurance, and people call me about their plan updates, they always ask me about which prescriptions I am taking. I tell them that I don't take any meds and they are astonished. They always say, "Not any?????" Uhhhh, yeah, not any.

I feel that the main reason I don't take a lot of meds is because I do try to stay away from doctors. No offense to doctors, because I know doctors take an oath to heal. But my philosophy is that doctors and pharmaceutical companies are in the business of sick people. That isn't to say that doctors want us to be sick, I just think that many times when we go in with this ache or that pain, prescribing the newest prescription drug on the market is what is expected from the patient. And some patients insist on being given 'something' to address their issues or they feel that their visit and complaints weren't validated.

But then I hear commercial after commercial that warn us with a laundry list of what can happen if we do take the drug they are hawking, ummmmm I mean advertising – all with lovely music playing in the background, that I assume is meant to distract us from what they are saying that their drug could do to us, by the guy who is talking so fast behind the lovely music, that you can't fully comprehend what is being said.

But these contraindications and warnings that should scare the hell out of anyone, seem to be continually ignored. And some warnings even say that you may die! And then some ads inform you that the very drug that they were 'pushing' just a few months ago – with the same lovely music in the background – that if you or a loved one took said medication, they are now advised that you should contact the law firm of XYZ for compensation. DUH!!! And yet, some people continue to ignore the warnings and choose to take the drug anyway. And THAT is why I just allow my own body to do as it was made to do and 'heal thyself'. AMEN to that!

What I mean by 'allowing my body to heal itself' is that I believe that we are able to heal sometimes without medicine or surgery in some cases. Of course, there are times that medications are necessary, but the conventional bias of the medical field seems to be that you have to have a procedure or medication to heal, when you may have healed without those meds just as easily.

I just recently did a bang up job on my own stomach. I had started a job that included standing on my feet for several hours a day. Well, my legs and feet started to ache and I began taking ibuprofen several times a day. That was a big No No for my tummy. It wasn't until my stomach started burning, that I realized what I had done. I had burned a hole in my stomach lining. Doofus me!

I tried to heal myself with holistic therapies and it helped some, but I did have to go to the doctor for a prescription to coat my stomach, so it would heal. So, I am not advocating never going to the doctor. Just be careful about what you are taking. And READ THE CONTRAINDICATIONS that come with your prescription. If it makes the hairs on the back of your neck stand up.....maybe you should rethink putting it into your system?

On a related subject, no one likes to think or be told that their pain is all in their head when they are the ones who are feeling pain. But when you think about it, the brain is what tells all of our senses what's up and what we're feeling. So it's not pejorative to say that something is in your head, because it actually is. We are finding now that there is a connection with the mind-body that we can tap into for healing as well.

So it follows then, that a lot of the time if we can take our focus off of our pain, through practices that help take our mind off of the pain, it can take the place of more drastic measures.

I know even for myself that when I may have had some kind of health malady that's bugging me, that as long as I focus on it, it will linger and grow larger. But sometimes if I go to work or go to the grocery or put my mind on something else, I will find that later on I'll think, wow whatever it was is gone now. And I find I am doing that a lot more now that I am getting older. LOL

Another 'not for sissies' part of the aging process is when you are forced to realize that you have less than a 'vital part' in the lives of your children, or the workforce, or any other place that you used to be a very vibrant and necessary part of society. The way you were when you were a mommy to your little ones or the boss of the business(s) you owned.

You feel invisible many times when you reach that 'certain' age. Once, you were managing life and a job and family, and now you only are managing which TV shows you will watch, and what you will have for supper. Or you find that you are just waiting for the next holiday for a family get together.

I do find myself at times questioning if my mind is as sharp as it used to be. And it most likely is not. But I tell myself that I'm probably just tired....or my mental Rolodex is full. For those of you who haven't reached that certain age yet, I realize that you don't have a clue what a Rolodex is. So, GOOGLE it. LOL

Lately, I find myself noticing the sagging skin and each new sign that old age is creeping up faster than I would like. The declining balance, memory and other maladies that we face in getting older is a nuisance. But maneuvering around the pesky nuisances is better than the alternative. And not dwelling on them is even a better idea.

If you are still reading this you are one of the lucky ones to be alive, and you can remind yourself that you could be one of the unfortunate souls that live in a nursing home. You probably shiver when you think of having to live in one of those places where you have visited friends or family members, and are just thankful it isn't you. YET!

And take all of the new technology we have to learn as we age. Like texting. I didn't like it at first, but if I wanted to 'converse' with anyone younger than myself, I had to get on board — or the keyboard. I do wonder though what other technology will come along in the future that will allow us not to have to communicate face to face ever again. In my opinion, I think the good old days were much better. We used to actually talk to each other. What a concept!

Of course you want your children to be self-sufficient and not 'need' you in the way that they did when they were children. But the realization that you aren't 'necessary' or crucial in their day-to-day life can cause you to feel sad at times. It really is a double-edged sword. On the one hand you feel obsolete and on the other hand, you are ecstatic that your children are doing so well that you aren't needed anymore.

I also feel that if parents would just realize that there is a time for parenting and a time to just be a parent, they would get along a lot better with their grown children. But it is hard to remember to keep quiet when you think it may help those you love. *Insert a Big, Looooong Sigh Here*

Another 'getting older' fact that we must be cognizant of is falling. And you probably will fall someday if you aren't very aware of your surroundings and your diminishing capabilities. It comes on slowly, but you find that one day you just don't have the same balance, equilibrium, or the steadiness that you always took for granted in your youth. It sort of creeps up on you — like Jack the Ripper, in a dark alley, with a dagger kind of way.

And even if you are lucky enough not to have landed in the aforementioned nursing home, you may still find that you will live your last years in one doctor's office after another. And probably being a nuisance to your grown children, which I personally never want to happen. Make that, I pray that will never be the case.

I have even begun a habit of keeping one elbow touching the wall whenever I am taking a shower these days. And I am always very careful about entering and exiting the bath as well. How embarrassing would it be to have to have the EMT rescue you - and you be naked? I'd rather die! Just kidding.....but it would be mortifying to say the least.

Not to be a downer (oops, too late?) but not facing the fact that you are not the spry young chicken that you once were can have some very serious repercussions. You could fall and break a hip and that can lead very quickly to the slippery slope of your demise. Cue the sad trombone sound of Debbie Downer fame. ♩♩ wah-wahhhhhh ♩♩

On a funnier note, I remember my Mom telling me to always wear clean underwear because you never know if you'll be in a car accident and you wouldn't want to be embarrassed. Well, when you get to be my age, you're always thinking about how you leave things that will be found when you're gone. I've found myself throwing out some things that I'd just die if anyone saw. But hey....I would already be dead, so there wouldn't be too much embarrassment – for me anyway! And don't bother asking me what it was that I threw away either. If I had wanted to be outed....I wouldn't have made the effort to throw it away in the first place. DUH!

One day you do look in the mirror though and think when the hell did I get this old? And immediately after thinking that – you say a prayer that you will live to be even older. And what's with the random hairs that take on a life of their own with crazy growth spurts, while the other places that used to have hair, stop growing? And the thinning that we do get is the hair on our scalp. And then we lose the fat from our hands and they become crepey-looking. And what about losing fat on the pads of our feet, or our forearms? That's where we lose fat????? Instead of losing it on our hips and thighs?? OY! There must have been a glitch somewhere in the human hardware planning.

I have always said that God made one mistake by not allowing us to go from being old to growing younger, instead of the way that it does play out. Like in the Benjamin Button movie, we would appreciate all of the little things we don't appreciate when we are young. We would wake up and a wrinkle would be gone and we'd be sooooooo happy. Or, our hair would thicken back up each day. Or, the color of our hair would become the vibrant, rich color that it was when we were young. And the aches and pains would subside with each passing day. And our waistlines! We'd actually have one again!! Oh, the things we would love to see happen. Hip, Hip, Hooray. Oh yeah, speaking of hips - our hips would work again and be slim and tight once more. Ahhhhhhh

Getting older though also reminds me of the beautiful sentiments expressed in the book The Velveteen Rabbit. One of the passages in the book lovingly articulates how it is to age: "*You become. It takes a long time. That's why it doesn't happen often to people who break easily, or have sharp edges, or who have to be carefully kept. Generally, by the time you are REAL, most of your hair has been loved off, and your eyes drop out and you get loose in the joints and very shabby. But these things don't matter at all, because once you are REAL, you can't be ugly, except to people who don't understand.*"

The reminder, in case you haven't faced it yet, is that you ARE getting older. Your first reminder may begin when we get that notice in the mail that we are now eligible for AARP. Or when you start getting emails that you may need Viagra or incontinence meds and pads. Or emails from dating sites for older people fill up your inbox. Smart Asses!!!

The people who send you these notices are probably from young people who think they will never need these 'reminders' one day themselves. Spoiler Alert: Your own version of those emails is just lurking around the corner, and you too will reach the age that you never thought you would become so quickly.

So, enjoy yourselves while you can still laugh without worrying about tinkling on your Depends pad. And now, all you youngsters, you've been fair and lovingly warned.

The upside of getting older is that you become wiser. Most times this 'wise-ness' is usually the result of having failed many times over. I truly believe that you learn a lot more from your failures than you ever do from your successes. It seems that we don't really learn until it hurts (us). So goes the saying about having to have a brick fall on our own heads before we 'get it'. I know for myself, that each 'failure' I have had has given me some of the most important lessons that life had to offer. And expanded my perspective more broadly each time.

I find that where older and younger generations are at opposite ends of the spectrum, is that as we age, we are looking back at all of the wonderful years we've had – and when we are young, we are mostly looking ahead for what's to come. But both of these ways of thinking leaves out fully appreciating our 'Now'.

The real secret to a happy life is to stay in the 'now moments' because that is really all that we have that is tangible and certain. And even 'Now' is very brief and passes by exceedingly fast.

I do see other people who are my age that appear to look older than I do. Or maybe I'm just fooling myself. But as long as we keep moving and keep up our appearance as well as we can, I think we will age better. Just look at Jane Fonda if you want to see someone who takes great care of themselves. I know people say that she's had work done, and has had plastic surgery, etc. But I say God Bless her! I would have those procedures done too if I had her money. And I don't see what all the fuss is about when people have 'work' done. If our car is in an accident, we have the dents fixed, don't we? And if our house needs painting, we paint it. So why should our cars and homes be more important to keep up than we are?

Another good thing about getting older is that you can be choosy about who you want to hang out with. You would think that by the time I had gotten to be the age that I am now, that I would have less chance of making really good friends. But that isn't true.

I met a wonderful new friend just a few years ago that I feel very close to. Her name is Diana and she is married to my husband's (and now my) good friend Stan. Let me tell you something for sure - it is truly a blessing when your husband likes your friend AND their spouse. Sometimes we can have a really good friend and our spouse can't stand their spouse, and vice versa. But Diana and Stan and Mike and I do love to get together when we have the chance, and we always have a blast and truly enjoy being in each other's company. The only problem is that we are all so very busy that it isn't nearly as often as we would like!

Diana is on a similar spiritual wavelength as I am. One time we manifested a trip to NYC to see the Christmas lights and decorations. At the time, neither of us thought it was possible because of our schedules and it being so close to the holidays. But we told each other that we had to walk to walk, instead of talking the talk about this manifesting stuff if we really wanted to make the magic happen. And we made it to NYC, visited our friend Lindy Lou and the other ladies who live up there, and we had a total BLAST!!!! Voila'. Easy Peasy Lemon Squeezy!

And I can't forget to mention our good friend Howard Fabian. Howard is the type of friend anyone would just love to have. He is always there when you need him, and you won't find a better, more loyal friend. Howard is proof that real friends aren't always measured by how long you've known them.

Mike and I have been blessed with the best friends anyone could ever wish to have. Mike's college buddies Bob Montgomery and Danny Isbell, still keep in touch with us, all these many years later. And their wives, Ann and Karen, are the bomb too.

We recently held our 3rd annual Brady's Heroes Charitable Foundation golf tournament, and if Bob and Ann hadn't flown down from Alabama to help us, we never would have been able to pull it off. And I mean that literally! Of course, Diana has always been there for us in helping with the tournament, and she and her daughter Natalie were a great help this year as well. These are the kinds of friends that don't wait to be asked if you need help. They just jump in with both feet and help!

CHAPTER 19

Understanding It All a Little Better

I've come to believe that although we think that we alone are choosing life, I feel that life is also choosing which encounters we will experience. Or at least that we are being guided to find our best life. But it's always up to us to choose. And with each decision we make, our lives go in that direction.

"Life is the Dancer and YOU are the Dance". That's a quote by my earliest 'teacher' Eckhart Tolle. I have to admit that I didn't understand the quote for many, many years. To me it means that Life, as the dancer, flows through us - - to whatever 'dance' we choose to vibrate to. The dancer makes the dance come alive! Sometimes the dance is a slow and easy waltz, and sometimes it's a tango.

"Allowing the truth of who you are—your spiritual self—to rule your life means you stop the struggle and learn to move with the flow of your life. You then realize that you don't live your life - - but life lives you". Remembering still, that we always have the option of Free Will that can change the direction of our life at any moment, if we choose to use it. I can now see my life's perspectives from both a younger me point of view and from the point of view of being older.

But the real meaning of life IS to live in the Now, because that is where life is happening - - NOW. Don't hurry your life along. Savor the special moments and memories. Those memories will keep you company one day.

I see it so often when people say they can't wait for Friday so that their weekend will begin. But we don't see that there is so much to enjoy while we wish our Monday's thru Thursday's away.

Now is the only time that we can truly 'make anything happen'. Yesterday is gone and tomorrow isn't promised.

Life can seem to be a struggle for us to keep our heads above water at times. But we must have a hand in changing what we don't like when it is showing up for us. Or ask for guidance to change what is appearing. This reminds me of the story about a nun, Tenzin Palmo, who was also an Englishwoman and the daughter of a fishmonger from London's East End, who spent 12 years alone in a cave 13,000 feet up in the Himalayas.

"She found herself snowbound in her secluded retreat during an avalanche that was precipitated by a storm. The situation seemed hopeless. For many hours she sat quietly, practicing meditation and observing her thoughts, her fears. She prepared herself for death. In the midst of her meditation, and with an internal state of great calmness, she heard a voice with a strong demand. "Dig!" it said. She did, and lived".

Sometimes all we need to do is to dig.

None of us has any true assurance of anything beyond this present moment. So I would suggest that we enjoy the ride and savor every moment along life's path. The journey is where all the best parts of life are experienced. The destination is the end of the line. So don't be in such a hurry to get there.

I look back on my own life now and I can see how I would never have met all the wonderful people along the way if I hadn't tried those things that turned out to be what is traditionally thought of as unsuccessful. But I wouldn't trade any of those relationships and experiences that we enjoyed from those choices. Those life lessons and the friends that we made, all helped me to make me who I am today.

And I can see now that in many of my life experiences, I was foregoing my Free Will and allowing myself to be the 'dance' so that I could experience the many situations that I needed for my own spiritual growth. I may not have known at the time that I was listening to the whispers of my Higher Inner Source, but I think that I was. We can always feel or sense when something is pulling us in one direction or the other. Sometimes we just take the path that our heads tell us to take, instead of listening to our guts.

It's commonplace how very easy it is to feel arrogant or complacent when everything is going great guns. But how we respond and react when the 'you-know-what' hits the fan is far better evidence of our character. Good or bad. In fact, our true character is better revealed by the way we handle adversity, much more than when everything is going great. I agree 100% with the sentiment that "Adversity doesn't change who you are – it REVEALS who you are."

I picture life as sometimes needing a metaphorical scaffold when things are out of our reach. But when we finish with whatever project that we needed the extra help with and it's accomplished, we take the scaffolding down and store it away until we need it again. We don't need the scaffolding to stay in place all the time, just for when we need a little help 'rising up'. This way, we can climb high, while knowing that we always have a support system close by if we need it. All the while, keeping in mind that we must leave the door open for the good things to come into our life.

However, these 'wise-up' lessons are meant for each of us to learn independently. No one learns from other people's mistakes. It's only when THEY make the mistake and THEY feel the burn, that will they 'get it'.

Many people just don't seem to possess the empath gene. If it isn't about them, then they don't give it much thought or care. GOOGLE says: 'Empathy is the experience of understanding another person's condition from the other person's perspective'. I feel the world would be a much better place if we could all see from other people's viewpoints. Like the Indian proverb about walking a mile in someone's moccasins.

I haven't always felt empathy towards others and their difficulties in the past as I should have. Years of self-discovery finally opened the floodgates for me when I allowed myself to remove the 'shell' that had surrounded my heart, which I can now see that I trying to 'protect'.

Writing this book has also allowed me to discover when and how I formed the many beliefs that I had. The catharsis in writing this book has been enormously liberating for me. And I am very grateful that I didn't leave this Earth School without being able to feel deeply about others and their stories. It is a gift that I cherish. I understand the term 'with all my heart' so much more clearly now.

Compassion is a good thing. And if you don't or can't feel compassion – try to uncover the reasons why you aren't feeling that way. It's the best and most loving thing you can do. For others and for yourself.

I also think it would be a good idea for it to be mandatory to have our ancestry checked with DNA kits like they have these days. I bet that many people who are biased, intolerant and prejudiced, would think differently if they learned that they had some of the very same blood in them as in those people they hate. Hmmmmmmmm. Wouldn't that make for a great reality show with the results shown on TV of the staunchest haters and bigots test results! Instead of, "You are not the father" – it could be - "You are not all white!!!" "Or you are not all black.....or whatever ethnicity you thought you 100% were."

The world population keeps growing larger, but the ability to care or be empathetic about others seems to be diminishing. And I often wonder why and how this has happened. Just what has made so many of us not care about our fellow man/woman as much as we used to?

We all have our own perspectives and perceptions about life. But our perspectives and perceptions can be faulty. How many times have you heard two people recount an incident, and have completely different opinions about what happened? Our conclusions are clouded by what we want to believe rather than what actually happened. And this also colors how we think and feel about each other.

The political climate of recent times is a good example of people believing what they want to believe. Even in the face of proof positive of an opposite truth. The latest 2016 campaign in politics has proven to have brought out the very worst in people – all over the world. I have never seen or heard so much meanness and hate expressed as I have in current years. I fear for my own grandchildren, for what kind of life they will experience if the pendulum doesn't start swinging back to a kinder, gentler way of being and feeling towards each other soon. And it all comes down to each persons' learned perspective. You see, we are not born hating anyone. Hate is taught.

When we feel 'separate' from others, we take on a 'me only or me first' attitude. It begins with feelings of fear and insecurity that make one feel that they must defend their stance, attitude and even political biases, or they won't feel as good about themselves as they would like; or as they have projected themselves to be. Then we gravitate to those who feel and think as we do. I believe this tribalism that we have found ourselves in, is a planned scheme to bring our democracy down, by despots who want to rule the world. It's a slippery slope, and I sometimes feel that our nation is in another Civil War; with brother against brother and other family members and friends against each other. Well played Russia. Well played.

Many times people only act in certain ways to garner admiration and even adulation. This usually leads to being disappointed because we should never compare our life to anyone else's. As I've said before, comparison IS the thief of joy.

But I think it must also be the human condition because even back when we were in kindergarten, there was an urgency to be first in line, first to be picked when we raised our hands to answer the teacher's question, and the awful dread of being chosen last for team sides.

Somehow, we were made to feel less than and felt that we must get to the head of the line, even if it meant pushing someone else out of the way.

Unfortunately, I know some obnoxious people who remind me of someone who must have felt that they weren't noticed enough when they were children. And it's not a pretty sight, nor is it very much fun to be around them. And don't we all know people like that?

Another good thing to remember so that we can keep on the right track is that when we put money above what we know to be right, we have essentially sold our souls. It's the same as prostituting yourself. The Bible says that 'the love of money is the root of all evil'. Many people think the Bible says that 'money is the root of all evil', but that is not correct. Money, in and of itself, cannot 'do' or 'be' evil – it's when wrongdoings and transgressions are done because of the LOVE of money that the trouble begins.

People end up feeling less than those who do have money and they begin to desire what their neighbors have. Then BAM, the snowball starts going downhill, building momentum, plowing over anyone in its way.

There's a very good reason "Thou shall not covet" made it into the Ten Commandments. To covet means to yearn to possess something that someone else has. When we are happy for others, good fortune seems to find its way back to us. However, we are not supposed to act a certain way, just for the reason that it brings something back to us. That is called a 'deal', and that just isn't how the You-niverse works.

CHAPTER 20

Do Unto Others

What does work for our best outcome is to be happy for our neighbor and fellow man/woman/child when they do well. It's like a story that I love, and explains this so well:

There was once a farmer who grew award-winning corn. Each year he entered his corn in the state fair where it won a blue ribbon. One year a newspaper reporter interviewed him and learned something interesting about how he grew his corn. The reporter discovered that the farmer shared his seed corn with his neighbors.

"How can you afford to share your best seed corn with your neighbors when they are entering corn in competition with yours each year?" the reporter asked.

"Why sir" said the farmer, "didn't you know? The wind picks up pollen from the ripening corn and swirls it from field to field. If my neighbors grow inferior corn, then cross-pollination will steadily degrade the quality of my own crop of corn. If I am to grow good corn, I must help my neighbors to grow good corn as well."

The farmer was very much aware of the connectedness of life. His corn cannot improve unless his neighbor's corn also improves. And as another saying goes, "One bad apple can spoil the whole barrel."

And so it is with our lives. Those who choose to live in peace must help their neighbors to live in peace. Those who choose to live well must help others to live well; for the value of a life is measured by the lives that it touches. And those who choose to be happy must help others to find happiness. As President Theodore Roosevelt so wisely said, "The welfare of each of us is bound to the welfare of all."

Another worthy maxim to remember is: 'to those who much has been given, much is expected'.

Just recently, there was a total eclipse of the sun. As the time for eclipse drew near, it was fun asking people if they were 'ready' for the eclipse, and to hear them say that they actually were. It was also very much fun seeing all the 'watch parties' on Facebook with all the people wearing their eye protectors and even some homemade boxes with pinholes in them to look through.

Some were lying in their pools, some on reclining chairs outdoors, and some were just standing and looking upward in awe.

But the common thread in all these scenarios was that no one was disagreeing about what they were experiencing. I think it just felt good to be enjoying something together – for a change – where there were no arguments, or sides, or biases. We all felt connected in a common experience.

Everyone was able to see and appreciate the majesty that is Mother Nature. No one was entitled to a better 'front row seat' because they could afford to buy a more expensive ticket. Funny how nature works, right? Totally impartial - - all the time.

It felt good to be a part of something much bigger than ourselves. And it put into perspective just how small it makes us look when we bicker and fight all the time.

It was good to realize that nature does her 'thing' for all of us the same - without favoritism or judgment. The moon and the sun shine on the sinner and the saint alike, the rich and the poor and the young and the old – without the judgment of who deserves it or not. This is called Grace. The rain doesn't fall on just one of us, or only on those of us who have the most. The rain falls and the sun shines equally on each of us to enjoy.

So, thank you to the sun and moon for your awesome display. It felt really nice to be in unison with everyone for a change. Even for a little while at least. And thank you to The All That Is for the guidance that's allowing me to awaken to these epiphanies.

There are so many things that unfold as we become what I and a lot of my 'woo-woo' friends call 'awakened'. To be awakened isn't about learning new things, it's about remembering why we came into this life experience in the first place. Awakening is about forgetting or UN-learning ideas that don't fit in with our conscious awareness anymore.

I know it can make people uncomfortable when they come across those who believe differently than they do. I realize that it's hard to reject the core beliefs we've had since childhood. Beliefs that are 'baked in'. And as anyone can imagine, it's impossible to un-bake a cake, when all of the ingredients have already been measured out, mixed, and then baked.

Not to mention the scorn you could feel from your church friends and family if you were to voice any doubts that you may have. It's very understandable then, that you would stay quiet about any questions you have. But there comes a time for many of us when the questions outweigh staying silent. Our inner spirit just revolts. Just as in the beautiful words of Anais Nin, "And the day came when the risk to stay tight in the bud was more painful than the risk it took to blossom".

My Mom used to take me to different denominations of churches on Sunday's when I was growing up. I like to say that I was raised a 'Visitor'. I can't tell you how many times we were introduced to the congregation as the new visitors. But I feel that by not being fully indoctrinated in any one religion, it allowed me to be more open-minded when I did begin my search to know about The All That Is.

My Dad did not come along on our church visits. Dad was raised Catholic in Italy, but when he read about the Inquisition of Spain through his self-teaching, he just quit the church all together because he said that he couldn't be part of any church that tortured and killed people who didn't believe as they said they should.

Did I mention that my Dad was a tad stubborn and opinionated about some things? Yeah, there was that about him too. But then again, aren't we all opinionated and stubborn when it comes to how we think and what we believe?

I wasn't knowledgeable or informed enough on these topics at that age to point out to Dad that you can't blame the behavior of some on a whole religion, creed, sex, or nationality. Some people still have a hard time with that concept.

If I may reiterate, feelings of separateness always cause great conflict. Divide and conquer is said to be 'the policy of maintaining control over one's subordinates or subjects by encouraging dissent between them'. It's the tool used to separate us, and to win power over the masses. I say don't fall for it my friends! And be aware when it feels like it's happening around you.

Although I was not raised solely in any one religion, I admit that I felt very fearful the first time I thought to myself that the whole virgin birth thing just didn't add up for me. I felt that I was going to 'burn in hell' - as I had heard promised a time or two in some of those various church halls that I had visited.

However, I do respect everyone's beliefs and I expect them to respect my right to believe the way I feel most comfortable believing as well. No harm, No Foul and Live and Let Live is my motto.

And I realize that it isn't easy for people to be the 'rebel' and question what has been taught and has been believed since they were children. But I never offer my thoughts on these things, except to those who may ask or in conversations with others who do think the way I do. Or in a memoir - like now!

A few years ago, I joined a gathering of like-minded people in a group called UnAsleep. I had begun listening to and watching some of UnAsleep's videos on YouTube and they really resonated with me. Then UnAsleep started a closed Facebook group and I joined it. I have to say that I have become closer to some of these people than to some people that I have known for years.

I had never discussed this group with Mike or Tracey, or anyone for that matter, about the friendships that I had made with some of the members in the group.

And all of these friendships were on online at the time. I had not met any of my new like-minded friends face-to-face. And many are from different parts of the world.

But one of the members, Linda, who I affectionately call Lindy Lou, and who I am very close to now, decided to have a get-together for anyone in the UnAsleep group that wanted to meet in person. I desperately wanted to go and meet them, but I had to tell Mike and Tracey that I was going. (Cue the Twilight Zone music again).

They both thought I was nuts! They said, "You're going to New York to meet with people you don't know??? And you're staying in someone's house that you've never met???? No way!"

But yes way!....I went. I felt in my gut that it was very important for me to get with others who shared what I had only been learning and understanding on my own. And it is lonely to keep what you are feeling concealed for fear that those you love will shun you or think that you're cray cray.

It turned out to be one of the best decisions that I have ever made in my life. It seemed as if everyone was as excited to meet each other as I was to be meeting them. I am very thankful to Lindy for that get-together. It was very generous of her, and just like who she is to be so kind, inclusive, and loving.

Lindy and I have met up several more times since that first wonderful gathering. She has come down to Florida several times and I have gone back to NYC to visit her. I feel that she is my Soul-Sistah! And there are many others from that group who I feel very close to as well.

And no, it's not a cult. And we don't all believe exactly the same about The All That Is. But we think enough alike to feel comfortable about discussing what we have come to understand along our own paths. It's like holding each other's hand as we travel down the Yellow Brick Road of understanding.

Please pass the Kool-Aid. Just kidding..............

Some of the original group even went on a trip to Denver one year to listen to another spiritual teacher. I won't name this teacher because he seems to be going through his own identity crisis right now. But he did have some enlightening thoughts and he did resonate with us at the time.

I think the problems he has is one that you see with a lot of 'gurus'. He just went too far in believing that he was bigger and more important than he actually was. But it seems to happen to many 'gurus' and religious zealots when they start to drink their own 'Kool-Aid'. It's called 'The Holy Man Syndrome'.

They suddenly begin to think that they are above everyone and everything else. The ironic part is that if we are all ONE, as many of them prophesize, then no one COULD be any better than the next person, right? I'm just glad that our group had the good sense not to go too far down that particular path. Thank goodness that I have always possessed the ability to take what does resonate with me and to leave what doesn't. And we do mostly know when something feels right and when it doesn't. I guess the reason some people stay with a particular guru/teacher, is that they just have too much invested in who they follow to ever admit out loud that something just feels off.

The group that went to that retreat were from all over the country. And I do feel they (Linda, Bethie, Pat, Erin, Heather, Brenda, Natalie, Carla, and Robert) will always be a large part of my spirit/soul posse, now and forever.

CHAPTER 21

A Skeptic's Guide From an Awakened Woo-Woo

OK, are you ready to dip your toe into the 'woo-woo pond' a little further? If you are, then you had better unfasten or loosen your 'thinking cap' too while you're at it, because you'll have to open up some space in there to let some new ways of thinking seep in. Here goes!

What I am going to offer now is my very own understanding of what The All That Is to me. You may agree with me, or it may scare you away. But this is just for you to reflect upon what are my own conclusions. You can throw out anything that you don't agree with, and keep any or part of what does resonate with you. You, of course, may have your own conclusions, and that is quite fine with me. No pressure from me for you to ever believe the way that I do. And none from you for me to believe your way either. OK? Sound fair? Deal.

My own awakening didn't come to me in one big lightning bolt strike. It came more in glimpses or flashes of what I have come to think of as knowing a-ha's. When I started giving up the 'need' to hold onto any stringent beliefs that I had built up in my life, the more the flashes of insight seemed to appear for me. And I figured out that as long as I was insisting that I see things in a set way, the more they stayed the same. That's the Free Will thingy at work, doing what we were promised, that we can do as we please with our lives.

So, how did our beliefs become what we think of as 'law'? I think that since we were born, we have been taught, cajoled, and to some degree, even a little brainwashed into thinking the way our parents think and believe.

Oh, and they were brainwashed by their parents too. It's just how beliefs perpetuate. And a belief is just a thought that you keep thinking anyway.

I get that religion is useful because without it, even more people would be doing all sorts of terrible things that lead to chaos, thievery, and even murderous acts. And the Bible does teach some great things about doing good deeds and treating others the way we wish to be treated.

But without the fear that religion teaches us about sinning, there would be no incentive to be good at all. Except for our conscience, which I don't feel many people are paying much attention to lately.

When the stories about The Beginning were shared waaaaaaay, waaaaaaay back in the day, most people didn't read and write, so analogy, metaphors, and symbolism had to be used in the telling of the stories.

I was listening to a video by Deepak Chopra on life, religion, and life after death one day and he described what I have now come to also believe is true. He put what I believe into the proper wording that just fit perfectly for me. He said, "God didn't create the Universe – God BECAME the Universe'. This has to be true if you believe the Bible that says God has no beginning and has no end - is now and forever shall be.

BAM – BAM – BAM – and BAM. This was truly a 'drop the mic' moment for me. It reminds me of the quote about a fish searching for water, while not realizing that it had been IN water all along.

What this means is that whatever you call Higher Source; be it God/Universe/Jesus/The All That Is – I believe this is Source energy. The SOURCE OF EVERYTHING AND EVERYONE. The energy that is IN everything and what everyone is made OF. Love Energy. Divine Intelligence = Loving Energy. WE are that Love Energy - incarnate.

And I believe that when we don't love, we are blocking this Love Energy from flowing as it is intended. And when we do love, we are allowing ourselves to see God is in every corner of every place and thing on Earth, and in the Universe. And in all of us as well. As it was always intended. Omnipresence personified.

This Love Energy only wants the very best for us. And is ALWAYS guiding us with UNCONDITIONAL love. But what some of us have a hard time comprehending is that unconditional means UN-conditional, with the emphasis on 'UN'. Never conditional. Got it? Good! WHEW!

So, if God loves us when we are good – then God must love us even, and in spite of, when we are 'bad' too, right? That's UN-conditional. Right? And if we use our free will to drive too fast and we end up in an accident, or walk in front of a car and get hurt or maimed or killed, or we take an overdose of pills to end this beautiful gift called Life – then in these ways, we are 'allowed' to do whatever it is that we want with our Gift of Life too, right? Because if we could only do what God wants us to do, then our will/desires would NOT be considered 'free', they would be.....wait for it - - conditional. Gotcha!

And what about the murderer who took the life of your loved one? God loves them too. Not because they murdered your loved one, but because nothing we could ever do could stop this Divine Love Energy from loving us. No exceptions. Remember?

If you can fully comprehend this, then you will able to stop blaming God for anything that goes wrong in your life. Ever again. Mostly because you will 'get it' that God IS all things and in ALL of us. And if that is the case, which I believe it to be, then everything must be included in the ONE. Good, bad, happy, sad, sick, healthy. It can be no other way.

But we CAN ask for guidance to show us the right path for our own journey because this does follow the principles of Free Will. When we ask – and we truly believe – then we will receive. The tricky part is the believing. Without that, the deal is off.

The concept of 'believing it to receive it' is something that I have mulled over and over in my mind for a long while. I have come to accept that what we experience comes from our thoughts becoming things. Yes, becoming. We think our lives up, one thought at a time. But people usually say, "I'll believe it when I see it" when it's actually the other way around. Wayne Dyer used to say that you have to believe it to see it, and he was absolutely correct.

Even the Bible says, "Truly I tell you, if you have faith as small as a mustard seed, you can say to this mountain, 'Move from here to there', and it will move. Nothing will be impossible for you." This doesn't mean that you actually move a mountain, it's a metaphor that means that what you believe will come to you – if you really and truly do believe.

But what we don't factor in, is that what we fear is drawn to us as well. Any doubt will cancel out what you want too. Doubt changes the trajectory of your reality. The Bible says, "Seek, and ye shall find; knock, and it shall be opened unto you." This is the promise that God will give whatever is needed to those who have the faith to ask for it.

But then you may say that you can't possibly believe that you are wealthy when you are having trouble making ends meet. THAT's the paradox. We have to have enough faith to NOT believe what we are seeing and experiencing. We have to picture our life the way we want it to be instead of what we are experiencing. Because the Universe brings to us what it is that we think about with great emotion, and believe it to be true.

However, we do seem to be able to believe the bad stuff more easily than the good stuff. We humans – Ermagherd!

Then the problems persist when we believe what we see. Then we believe what we see and it keeps appearing precisely because we believe what we are seeing. GAHHHHH. I know it's confusing and I haven't gotten it down to a tee yet myself. As the famous genius Albert Einstein said, "Reality is merely an illusion, albeit a very persistent one." And he also said, "Life is a presentation of choices. Wherever you are now, exactly represents the sum of your previous decisions, actions and inactions". I guess it's easier to 'get it' if you're a genius and a theoretical physicist. Ha!

When I hear the word 'realize', I think of it as real eyes, or conversely real lies. We think that what we see with our real eyes is our REAL- ity. But we can actually change our reality at any time if we truly trust that we can. This is Law of Attraction in action, providing us with what we believe and feel with great emotion. Good and Bad.

LOA (Law of Attraction) is how we manifest everything, every minute of our lives. We draw to us what we believe – and how we feel about what is going on in our lives. And the intensity of our emotions about how we feel will bring us what we are thinking about even faster.

But don't forget that this means the good stuff AND the bad stuff. So, be careful with your thoughts.

So, since this is how our lives unfold, we should think and feel FROM the place of what we want, instead of thinking OF how we want our lives to look. We must act as if what we imagined and wished for has already materialized for us. Like visualizing being on a cruise to some exotic place. FEEL what that would feel like, and you will be in THAT vibration, and it will materialize for you more quickly. You can't be in two different vibrations at the same time. So pick the best feeling vibration at all times.

There is nothing that is real in our life that wasn't imagined first. Every discovery was imagined first. Every trip that you planned was imagined first. Every meal that you ate was imagined first. Every EVERY-THING....was a thought that you imagined first. Then the 'magic' of manifesting happens somewhere in the middle....between thinking about it becoming....and it actually appearing in our lives.

Scientists and quantum physics now tell us that matter is the principle of potentiality. Form is the principle of actuality. I read an article in Science News that explained this to some degree: [Considering potential things to be real is not exactly a new idea, as it was a central aspect of the philosophy of Aristotle, 24 centuries ago. An acorn has the potential to become a tree; a tree has the potential to become a wooden table. Even applying this idea to quantum physics isn't new. Werner Heisenberg, the quantum pioneer famous for his uncertainty principle, considered his quantum math to describe potential outcomes of measurements of which one would become the actual result. The quantum concept of a "probability wave", describing the likelihood of different possible outcomes of a measurement, was a quantitative version of Aristotle's potential, Heisenberg wrote in his well-known 1958 book Physics and Philosophy. "It introduced something standing in the middle between the idea of an event and the actual event, a strange kind of physical reality just in the middle between possibility and reality."]

So, the trick is to stop believing what you see, and replace it with thoughts and feelings of great emotion to what it is that you do want –

and then the Universe has no other choice than to bring it. Easier said than done – I know. But, I have had some success with this practice on a smaller level. And only after much practice I might add. It doesn't always work, because I suspect that some things are just too big of a jump for me (or you) to believe. This is what I call my self-induced barricade that I've somehow placed around what I want, and that keeps me from getting it. And our ingrained and sub-conscious beliefs about certain things are blockages too. Find those blocks, rip them out, and it's free sailing from there on out.

I know in my own case, some of my beliefs have been so rooted in what I have thought for so long that it's very hard to uproot those beliefs. The other part of this process consists of unpeeling those beliefs to find where they began. I understand exactly what old Albert meant by 'reality being an illusion, albeit a very persistent one!'

I had read the book The Secret when it came out a few years ago; along with half the world I think. The book explains this concept. Everyone who read it thought that they could have that expensive car or that big mansion, or......whatever XYZ they were hankering for if they just followed the book and/or movie instructions. But when their wishes didn't come to fruition, I guess they just thought it was a hoax.

I don't think it's a hoax though. I just think that you have to practice, practice, practice, and then one day, something will happen that you have been thinking or hoping for, and you get a little confidence about your manifesting abilities. Then you go on to try bigger things....and so on. This allows us to think of the things we want without resistance. Our reality comes to us through the path of least resistance. But there are other components to manifesting too that keep our manifestations from materializing. I will share those with you a little later on.

I do recall an occasion when my believing did manifest something very quickly for me. It happened one time when I had been reading a book on a flight down to visit my daughter Tracey. The book shared instructions on how to change something you didn't want in your life by thinking it away!

I was living in Tennessee at the time and would come down to Florida and visit Tracey and John and their new, sweet baby daughter Samantha every so often.

When I got to Tracey and John's, I started feeling very sick. My head was pounding, I felt nauseous and was even a little feverish. I was so upset because I didn't want to be the cause of getting anyone else in the house sick. And I surely didn't want to have to stay away from my beautiful granddaughter Samantha while I was visiting.

So Tracey went to the drugstore and brought back some cold pills for me. I took them and then I remembered the book I had been reading on the flight down. I got up from the bed and took the book out of my luggage. I turned to the part that described what you do to change your current reality. It said that you close your eyes and picture a bright white light over your head. You then visualize that light going down through your body and having it cleanse anything that is unwanted in your body. You continue to picture each cell of your body being healed. Then you see the light take the illness or whatever it is you want to be rid of, out through your feet and then vaporizing, so it won't be around at all for anyone else to come in contact with. You do this several times, all the while seeing the cleansing light going up and down and out of your body. And each time you visualize it, you sense yourself feeling better.

Now I know this may sound really and truly woo-woo to you, but sometime during the process of seeing the bright light moving up and down and out of my body, I fell asleep. And I swear to all that is Holy, when I awoke the next morning I was completely well! And I know that no over-the-counter cold pill could have made such a miraculous recovery for me in such a short amount of time.

That experience made me more of a believer than I ever could have been, had it not happened to me personally. I SWEAR!! I'm sure Tracey remembers it too and can attest to it that I'm not crazy. Well, not totally crazy anyway. I think she does think that I'm a little too woo-woo for her liking at times. But that's OK. This is my Storyboard and she has her own. LOL

Since that time. I have wondered many times why it happened so easily for me on that particular occasion, and other things that I have tried to manifest, seem to escape me. I think that in that instance that I really and truly believed what the book said I could do. There was no hidden resistance at all because I felt strongly that I wanted to be well and that I wanted to be able to hold and cuddle Samantha while I was visiting. It just reinforces for me that what we truly believe when we ask (without resistance) - - does find its way to us.

And just very recently, I again had a remarkable 'healing' experience that I attribute to this belief that I could be healed by this manifesting tool.

I had gone to meet my daughter and granddaughter at the mall after work one day. I remember my ankle feeling a bit sore but I didn't give it too much thought at the time. Pretty quickly, my ankle really and truly began hurting me while we were walking around the mall. When I got home, I proceeded to put ice on it and I elevated it too. Then I switched to applying a cloth that I had soaked in Epsom salt water on my ankle area. But the ankle stayed swollen and it was throbbing. It was more of an aching, like a toothache would feel.

I kept thinking that I may have broken it, or that maybe I had a hairline fracture. At my age, it's not uncommon for our bones to be brittle enough so that I may have caused a small fracture by twisting my foot or something. I went to bed and it was hurting so much that I was getting even more concerned that I had in fact broken or fractured my ankle.

I had to work for the next 3 days in a row and I just couldn't miss work because I was the only one who was working the day shift at my job. So, I closed my eyes and did my healing light ritual thingy again. I kept visualizing the light going up and down my leg and around and around my ankle and taking the pain out through my foot. I told myself that I must believe it for it to work. I finally did fall asleep and when I woke up the next morning – voila', no hurting ankle, no swelling and only the tiniest bit of tenderness. But I could walk without hobbling like I was doing the night before. And by the end of my work shift that day, I had forgotten all about the throbbing pain that I had been feeling the night before.

So, you can believe it or not – but it sure did work for me. I know it could be said that I had sprained my ankle and the ice and Epson salt relieved the pain in my ankle. I may be inclined to agree with you, except that overnight is a bit of a stretch for anything to heal. I had GOOGLED it the night before to see what I could expect, and it said that it takes anywhere from 5 days to 4 months for a sprained ankle to heal – depending on the severity of the sprain. You can ask my husband to verify how sore my ankle was too because he was as worried about it as I was. But it doesn't matter who believes me – I BELIEVED ME and I ignored what was seeming to be my reality and chose to change that reality. And that is all it takes for the healing light procedure to work!

The mind is a powerful instrument and it has been proven over and over again that our mind can trick the body into thinking it is sick. So the reverse should also work too, right? We should be able to think ourselves well too. Think of the placebo effect. Studies have been made where half of the patient groups were given medicine for a particular illness and the other half were given a placebo. The half that received the 'dummy' pill felt better too, just as the half that received real meds did.

The medical field is not quick to connect any health issue to the sane mind. But there was a doctor who changed some very famous peoples' minds, and some of his medical colleagues' minds as well. His name was Dr. John E. Sarno.

[Sarno's most notable achievement is the development, diagnosis, and treatment of tension myoneural syndrome (TMS), which is currently not accepted by mainstream medicine. According to Sarno, TMS is a psychosomatic illness causing chronic back, neck, and limb pain which is not relieved by standard medical treatments. He includes other ailments, such as gastrointestinal problems, dermatological disorders and repetitive-strain injuries as TMS related. Sarno states that he has successfully treated over ten thousand patients at the Rusk Institute by educating them on his beliefs of a psychological and emotional basis to their pain and symptoms. Sarno's theory is, in part, that the pain or GI symptoms are an unconscious "distraction" to aid in the repression of deep unconscious emotional issues. Sarno believes that when patients think about what may be upsetting them in their unconscious, they can defeat their minds' strategy to repress these powerful emotions; when the symptoms are seen for what they are, the symptoms then serve no purpose, and they go away. Supporters of Sarno's work hypothesize an inherent difficulty in performing the clinical trials needed to prove or disprove the diagnosis, since it is difficult to use clinical trials with psychosomatic illnesses].

My husband is very good at manifesting things too. He isn't as woo-woo as me, but the reason he manifests what he wants is that he believes that he can get the XYZ that he wants. Like getting in to see someone that he doesn't have an appointment with. Or getting into a sporting event that is sold out. Or winning at every slot machine that he has ever sat down at to play. I've seen him do it time and time again.

One time Mike won thousands of dollars at a casino in Mississippi. Every slot machine he sat down at hit big. He was with a friend that day who can corroborate this too. Mike said that a woman that worked at the casino had said she saw a red bird on his shoulder when they got there. When Mike asked what that meant, she said it meant that he was going to win big that night. His friend asked if she saw a red bird on his shoulder and she said she didn't see any color bird on him! And she was right. Mike won big and his friend didn't win anything at all.

What differentiates Mike and most other people is that he just thinks he is going to win. Most people say that wonder how much they are going to lose at the casino, and they even say that they are bringing X amount of money to lose (or donate)! And Mike always wonders how much he is going to win.

The family joke in our house is that every time we go anywhere in the car, there is always a parking spot right in front of the place we are going. Mike just expects to find a spot right in front. And he always does. Even during the holidays, when the parking lots are chuck-full. We always laugh and say, "Look, there's Brady's parking spot."

Can you think of a time that you may have mentioned or thought of say, a red car? Then everywhere you look you see red cars. Or you may think that you haven't heard from someone in a while, and then you get a call or text from them right out of the blue! It's just like that. You think it - and there it is. The reason more of the mundane shows up more quickly for us is that there is no resistance to those things. The more we are resistant to a thought, the harder it is to manifest. It's the path of least resistance again.

The reason that is so, is that the Universe hears how we feel, not what we say. Remember I explained earlier that if we have a hidden belief stuck somewhere in our subconscious, it works like a roadblock that's in the way of what we think we want.

I know that this is a concept that's a hard one to grasp about our reality. As I said before, we tend to believe what we see. And why wouldn't we? Well, a good reason would be so that we could change something in our 'now' that we don't want there.

For example: Say you have a friend or co-worker, or lover, or spouse who is acting in ways that you wish that they wouldn't. So, you say to yourself, or heaven forbid to other people, how rotten they are and spell it out how awful they are in dreadful, visceral detail. Guess what? They don't have any choice but to BE or ACT the way you have already pictured them to be. Get it? You've put them in a box that they can't get out of it as long as you see them that way. Your wish IS your command.

Are you getting it yet? And this is not a judgment of those who can't see it yet, because it took me a while to understand how it all works too. And I still forget sometimes, and it takes me becoming uncomfortable while I'm marinating in the 'negative stew' I have put myself in before I remind myself to 'snap out of it!' We are creatures of habit after all. Doggone it!

So, the trick is to envision what you want to manifest in your life, while you ignore what is going on in your life. And people may say that you aren't in touch with reality, right? And I say, RIGHT ON, hallelujah, hot damn, and AMEN! Finally......you're on your way to becoming 'awake' and manifesting the life you want, instead of the life you don't want.

However, if you do like how your life is unfolding.....then carry on as you were. But remember that it's only as good as you believe it is...for as long as you believe it!

But.....and there's always a 'but' right? You may then ask why I (meaning Shirley) am not wealthy. Why did so many unfortunate things happen in my life if I'm so smart about how all of 'this stuff' works?

Well, I'll tell you. These things called 'blocks' that I mentioned earlier can make it difficult for us to see our way clearly to attaining our goals. These blocks are sub-conscious beliefs that we have, that are contrary to what we think we want. They are also known as Shadow Beliefs. And I obviously still have some shadow beliefs that I need to uncover. I've never said that I knew it all. And that's why I continue to search for answers.

For example: Say you would love to be more comfortable in how much money you have. But you had heard from your parents while you were growing up that money was hard to come by. Or that 'rich' people weren't good people, or that 'money doesn't grow on trees'. Or maybe it is something as simple as deep down, you don't think you are worthy of having a comfortable life. So your ingrained concept about money is that somehow money is 'not good'. Then all of those beliefs turn into blocks that keep you from manifesting a lot of wealth for yourself. And each negative thought is a seed that you are planting, and each time you think the thought, you are 'fertilizing' it, and it will grow and grow, until it is firmly planted in your mind.

Conversely, when you do try your hand at manifesting, think of what you want, with great enthusiasm, then put it out into the universe and then go on about your life – all the while, expecting it to appear. Don't keep worrying about it day in and day out. That would be analogous to planting a seed in the ground, and coming back every day, then taking the seed out of the ground, just to see if it has grown any. That would just be dumb, right?

Dr. Bruce Lipton is a scientist who says that our lives are run by the subconscious mind; and what Osho called the unconscious mind. Lipton says science shows that the subconscious runs our life 95 – 99 % of the time, every single day. And the subconscious mind is much more powerful than the conscious mind – in fact, over a million times more powerful as an information processor.

He says the reason that positive thinking only does not work, is because it's done with the conscious mind. And the conscious mind is not what is running our lives.

"And where is our conscious mind in all this? That tiny part that is supposed to be there for at least 1% of the day?" asks Lipton? "Well, it is there when we consciously use our creativity to work on a particular issue or project. But when we are not using it, what does it do? It daydreams!! It wanders off into the future or the past, and thus becomes unconscious, according to Osho. When it is somewhere else, it is not observing the unconscious mechanisms that are actually in this moment, running our behavior. So, not only are we unaware of when our unconscious tapes are playing, we don't even have the ability to use our conscious minds to become aware of and observe the mechanisms of the unconscious".

"The subconscious mind, says Lipton, is like a tape player – it just goes on playing the same old tapes we learned in early childhood. Those tapes are the messages we picked up mostly from our parents, or from anyone else who was very influential for the first six years of our lives. Most of the tapes run along the lines of, 'You are not good enough'; 'You don't deserve'; 'Other people are better than you'; 'You are not acceptable or respectable as you are; You have to be better.'

Lipton says "you have to learn how to use the Stop button on the tapes instead of the automatic Play button. And then change the tapes".

Osho said that the through meditation, we can 'watch the mind'. Meditation is the act of watching the mind, without getting involved in allowing the 'tapes to run in the background' on a continual loop.

Anando is the founder of the international personal discovery organization, Life Trainings, which is devoted to helping people realize their hidden potential, their resources, and shows people how to bring more awareness into their lives. She says that "whether these messages were given to us directly or indirectly, they are what we picked up from the way we were treated, and those messages went into our innocent unconscious minds where they became our truths. And then the tape player started replaying those messages any time we were in similar situations, and we acted accordingly. In other words, we started living in a vicious cycle where we went on proving those negative ideas about us were true, thus making them even stronger. And it still happens today! We still continue to sabotage our attempts at happiness, success, love, etc. We are just not aware that we are doing it ourselves, because it is, well… unconscious".

So, do keep going back and ripping out those false beliefs up by the root. And that isn't always easy to do. It takes a lot of time and searching within. Especially if we have never even wondered where our beliefs started to begin with.

And another component to manifesting something that seems elusive is that the experiences that we have may be a part of our 'Soul Contract'. The agreement we made before we 'dropped into' this Storyboard. This also plays a major role in our 'script'. But the good news is that we are the director, producer, scriptwriter AND actor in our storyline. So we can rewrite it any time we want to.

This is where the Free Will option comes into play again. It's kind of like a 'get out of jail free' card. But that has a catch to it as well.

Dang……right?

Our souls are always growing and expanding with the lessons we wanted to learn. And if we change directions this go round, we will have to learn the lessons another time. So even if you change your 'script', you will still have to check off all of the lesson boxes eventually.

But the good news is that we are all in this for eternity, and there are plenty of 'lifetimes' to get it all right and learn all of the lessons.

Would I suggest checking off the boxes of lessons as quickly as possible? Damn Skippy. Because it would seem to make our life experiences go a lot smoother if we could get the 'lessons' for the enrichment and enhancement of our souls out of the way earlier rather than later. It would also be helpful if we had a Lesson Plan. But life doesn't come with a syllabus. And the rules are so strict so that the laws of the You-niverse will work the same for everyone – every time!

There is also the 'veil of forgetting' that comes into play as we live out our Storyboard. It keeps us from remembering and seeing everything all at once. And not until we are 'ready', will we understand it all. There's a legend that an angel touches a baby's upper lip when they are coming into this world, leaving the indention there that we all have. This touch was thought to allow us to forget our previous lives.

Those of us who do ask the tough questions of ourselves can feel the veil thinning. We can glimpse 'shapes and images' that are on the other side of the veil. It is furthering the process of UN-learning much of what we were spoon fed all throughout our life.

CHAPTER 22

Circling the Drain Years

You know you're getting old when you keep receiving cremation or funeral ads in your email account. I just delete them as quickly as I come across them. There's no sense dwelling on morbid things, right?! I just figure that I don't have to worry about that right now. And actually, I won't ever have to worry about it, because I'll be dead when the time comes for those decisions to be made.

The only thing I have discussed with my husband and daughter is that I want to be cremated. I know our souls leave the instant we die, so it doesn't matter what we do with the remains (our meat suits). It's how people remember us that matters.

You don't have to go to a gravesite or any special place to show love, or to remember, and honor your loved ones who have transitioned. They are always with us in our hearts and memories.

The thought of 'circling the drain' may sound a little grisly for a woo-woo like me to be discussing. Someone who promotes life as going on for infinity. But to me, that phrase is pointing to the premise that we never consciously know when that last slurp will take us down the drain – this go 'round I mean. That is until we do know. *Wink*

On some level I feel that we do know when we are going to leave this earthly existence. I just don't think we know it (or remember) until the very moment that we do decide to check out permanently comes. It just makes sense to me that when we came into being – and made our 'soul contract', we must have included when we agreed to exit as well. Right?

I know a lot of us have heard of instances where people did seem to choose when they were going to die. Like the couples that had been married for over fifty years and die a day apart. Or like my Grandma Maudie. She had suffered from cancer and was bedridden at home for some time. We even had a hospital bed for her in Mom's house, and my Aunt Jackie graciously, lovingly and beautifully took care of her for as long as she could so Grandma could stay at home as long as possible.

We finally did have to admit Grandma into a nursing facility so she could receive pain medication that we were unable to administer ourselves for her comfort. She was in a coma the last week of her life, but my mom 'told her' that her beloved son, Uncle Bill, was going to be coming down to say goodbye to her.

So Uncle Bill came down from Detroit and got there about 2 in the morning, after driving straight through all night. Uncle Bill held Grandma's hand and said I love you to her and told her that she could let go now. And she waited until everyone had left to go home to get some sleep and then she did let go and left this earthly plane – on her own terms and her own timeline.

And then there was my Mom. She made her transition years later in a hospital after she had suffered a massive stroke. She was also in a coma for days. I was at her bedside day and night. Mom had always told me that she didn't want to be left in a vegetative state if what finally did happen to her ever did happen. But she also told me that I had better be sure she had no chance of ever coming out of it.

I had asked her doctor, who she loved and trusted completely, if Mom had any chance of recovering. He assured me that she did not. As an only child, it's a more difficult decision to have to make alone about the life and death decisions concerning your Mom.

Then one day I left to go home to shower and change clothes before coming back to Mom's room, and she had passed before I returned. I know in my heart that she made the decision herself to transition, so that I wouldn't have to, and also so I wouldn't have to be there when she did transition. Moms do things like that for their children. Even things that we think are impossible. And so do Dads.

Mom had been dealing with macular degeneration for several years and it was very hard on her. She had always been fiercely independent, and not being able to drive anymore, or to barely be able to see to get around was demoralizing for such a strong woman as she had always been.

Mike and I had been talking about moving to Tennessee and had asked Mom to come with us. Mom said she didn't want to leave her doctors, and there were several. I told her that Memphis had excellent doctors too but she said she wanted to stay in Florida, in her own home.

In the meantime, Mom's sister Maggie had moved in with her. They would sit or lie on the twin beds in Mom's bedroom and watch TV all day. And reminisce about their youth.

During this period of time, Mike and I had moved about 15 miles west of Mom's house, so Aunt Maggie's daughter Cheryl would check in on Mom and Aunt Maggie (her Mom) each day.

Cheryl would go to the store for them if they needed anything and since she lived so close, she was always very generous with her time and care. I would visit a couple of times a week and would take Mom to her doctor appointments, but having Cheryl look in on them each day was a blessing for sure.

Sadly, Aunt Maggie did pass and I know Mom missed her and the wonderful closeness that they had and the chance to share the last while that they lived together. Just like when they were kids. They told me they would laugh a lot and cry a lot, and remember their years together. I know they enjoyed every day that they did get to be together. It was truly a gift for each of them.

So, why don't we remember the agreement we made before dropping into this life? It has to do with the 'veil' I mentioned earlier that allows us to forget the agreement we made. Because if we could remember what we had agreed upon, we would probably try to make deals with ourselves when things got too tough. Or tweak the outcomes. So human of us, right? But this forgetting is evidence that our higher self is a lot smarter than our earthly self.

Another reason for forgetting our past 'drop in's' might be that we choose to start fresh, without any preconceived perceptions. Since the premise of time is really not relative, time doesn't really come into the equation. We know that while we are in the choosing part of the journey, that this is just one scene out of our whole Life Play. I know I skipped pretty quickly over the idea of 'time' not being a relative thing earlier. So in as few words as I can share, without losing you all together –"Time" is just a tool that [we] use to keep everything neatly in our linear concept of 'Now'. So that our human minds can grasp it all. And it's really a hard concept to perceive because our human minds are not wired to think differently than what we actually see in the physical.

If you believe in the Big Bang Theory, when everything was originally and neatly tightly bound in a 'ball' of perfection and order, over 13 billion years ago, and then KABOOM - there it and all of [us] 'began' then it's understandable why [we] humans have a need for order rather than disorder to make us feel comfortable. It's to get back to that place in 'time' when it all began, when everything was once perfectly perfect.

One would think that after all this 'time' that the universe would be slowing down. But it is actually expanding more rapidly. We can only imagine, or not, what life will be like in 100 billion years from now, when Earth is so far from the other galaxies that future humans will find that they won't be able to see Earth, even with the strongest telescopes imaginable. And we will all be explained away as just another era of humans, much like the caveman has been explained to us. More Twilight Zone Music please

But if you want to look it up and have it explained much more eloquently than I ever could, GOOGLE: Arrow of Time, Physics of Time and Entropy of Time. As the genius Danish physicists Niels Bohr said, "If quantum mechanics hasn't profoundly shocked you, you haven't understood it yet." (Raising my hand Dr. Bohr about the not fully understanding it all).

Many of us have come to accept, as Pierre Teilhard de Chardin offered, "We are not human beings having a spiritual experience; we are spiritual beings having a human experience." So it stands to reason that as spiritual beings, we come from a non-physical world, who know from that basis that [we] are infinite. And it takes the fear out of making any wrong choices. Because it's just a scene on our current Life Storyboard, right?

We knew that we were coming into each of our life experiences to expand our awareness. And that the experiences would be for the never-ending expansion of our soul. And how do we know if we are 'on the right track'? If it feels good, then we are on the right track. If it doesn't feel good, then we are moving away from what serves us. Learning to listen to our 'inner knowing' can lessen the crappy situations that we can sometimes get tangled up in.

About those crappy situations and what you can do about them? As long as you marinate in the feeling of not liking what you are experiencing, the longer you will stay in that place. Why? Because as I said before, the YOU-niverse mirrors back to us exactly what we focus on and what we resist – persists. It's all part of the perfect little 'game' that we all play, all the time, never realizing that we are the producer, director, and script writer of every life situation that we experience.

Think you can't manifest? Spoiler Alert: every situation and experience that you have, started as a thought. So, we are manifesting all the time. It's the waking up and deciding to brush our teeth, taking a shower and having some coffee. We do these things easily because we don't have any resistance to them and we expect to do these things. Manifesting something takes the path of least resistance. Remember those annoying blocks I spoke of earlier? They are everywhere. We just have to search them out and get rid of them. (She says casually). But as I also said before, it isn't as easy as just saying you want to discover what your blocks are. You have to go 'within' and search for them!

CHAPTER 23

Author? Check – Director? Check – Actor? – YUP, Check!

This brings me to the concept that our lives are being written BY us. Over the years we have heard hints about how this is so. We hear things like: (1) chapter and verse as it applies to knowing every detail about something in particular (2) The Book of Life, where it is said that God records the names of every person who is destined for Heaven or the World to Come (3) when someone says they closed a chapter on a part of their life (4) and when we say that we are making a fresh start, we say we are turning the page. Never thought of that now did ya'? Or if you have thought of these things, then you HAVE been listening to the whispers! Congratulations!!

All of these idioms point to how we are the authors, artists, and characters in our own stories. Many of these 'hints', 'whispers' and 'clues' are all around us. Some of us fit the puzzle pieces together and others never do, or at least they take a little longer to do so.

I didn't 'get it' either for many, many years and I can't tell you what made me 'get it' or why I finally did 'get it' when I did. I do think it has something to do with 'God's Grace' – which is said to be the unmerited and unearned influence of the Divine. Although I don't believe that this Love Energy, which I deem to be God, would give favor to one and not the other. I just think that it is always available to everyone. Some of us receive it when we least expect it. But I think it always comes when we ask for it. But understanding it only comes when we are ready to fully comprehend what The All That Is, is.

I realize that this way of thinking scares some people. It scares them so much that they will attack anyone who believes this way. And I sense it has to do with fear. THEIR fear that what they have believed all of their lives may not be completely accurate. I know that is a hard 'pill to swallow'. Somehow, the person with a different perspective from what a lot of other people think must be crazy! Heck, look what they did to poor Jesus!

But I say, why can't the person with a different perspective possibly be onto something? You know, like the scientists from a long time ago who argued that the earth was not flat? They got a lot of flak and criticism too because anyone could see that the earth was flat! Just look out the window. There are no downward curves when you look at the horizon! And it's very difficult to talk people out of what they think they are observing with their own eyes.

Those scientists who were saying the earth was round were even being called crazy. But, voila' – it's now a recognized truth that our planet truly is round. And this came to be because we had the technology to get far enough out to SEE that the earth was indeed round. Perspective at its best! All I say is that we should keep an open mind, because a closed mind never lets anything in that may be true as well.

And what about the Salem Witch Burnings?????? Yikes, look at what they did to those young girls who spoke of their beliefs that were different from the masses: "The infamous Salem witch trials began during the spring of 1692, after a group of young girls in Salem Village, Massachusetts, claimed to be possessed by the devil and accused several local women of witchcraft. By September 1692, the hysteria had begun to abate and public opinion turned against the trials". "Some historians believe that the accusation by Ann Putnam Jr. suggests that a family feud may have been a major cause of the witch trials. At the time, a vicious rivalry was underway between the Putnam and Porter families, one which deeply polarized the people of Salem. Citizens would often have heated debates, which escalated into full-fledged fighting, based solely on their opinion of the feud".

Now THAT is taking one's beliefs to a whole other level!!!! And it is still occurring today, evidenced by the political rhetoric spewed in the 2016 election. It always amazes me how people will fight to the death, or kill someone else, for not having the same beliefs or political slant as they have. If you ask me, THAT is the definition of cray cray!

But back to manifesting. The thing to do if you don't especially like your current 'reality' is to focus on how you would want your 'Now' to actually appear. Visualize how it would feel to experience XYZ. Bask in that feeling. Envision it with great gusto! And when you do get into THAT groove, the Universe just puts the pedal to the metal and VROOM.......you are now going at hyper speed and on your way to Ah-hhhhh-Land.

Remember, you are the author, director and actor, aren't you? And as Paul Coelho famously wrote in his fantastic book The Alchemist, "When you want something, all the universe conspires to help you achieve it".

And my daily 'Notes from the Universe' describes it like this:

[BE there, Shirley. Go there now and never leave. Imagine that your dreams have already come true. Live your life from that mindset. Predicate your behavior on that reality, not the illusions that now surround you. Filter every thought, question, and answer from there. Let your focus shift and be born again - because dwelling from, not upon, the space you want to inherit is the fastest way to change absolutely everything.

See the difference? The Universe]

But there is a stipulation though. Yeah, I know. There always is. Just remember not to allow any doubt to sneak into your thoughts while you are imagining and writing your script of how you want your 'Now' to be. Because as I have offered previously, just like popping a soap bubble with your finger, you will dissolve your beautiful visions and manifestations in their tracks. If you truly believe that what you are imagining cannot occur, it won't. POOF! Game over!

It's like the people who say, "I'd love to win the lottery, BUT....I'm just not lucky". BAM, you just changed your vibration of being a winner to being the same old loser you feel you always were.....with just that one negative thought.

Or the people that are always complaining about being sick. BAM.....those thoughts that you are always sick are KEEPING you sick. Why? Because you do believe that you are always sick. The Universe doesn't hear your words as much as what you believe.

Or the people who say, "I am always living paycheck to paycheck." Guess what? Yup.....and you always will as long as you think you will. That's how the game is played Peeps! If you want a different outcome – then think different thoughts, and then the odds of the game change in your favor. PERIOD!!!!

Are you thinking that sounds too unrealistic? Well, if you like the reality you are experiencing right now, then keep thinking the thoughts you are thinking. If your reality isn't all that 'smack', then not being realistic sounds pretty good to me!

And if people say that you are out of your mind, then I say hot damn, you've made it out of the doldrums and into the life of your dreams. Remember that getting out of our minds is the trick to getting what we want!

Abraham-Hicks explains it this way. When you are worrying about what you don't want, you are focusing on that, and keeping yourself in the place of 'not liking where you are'. This keeps you stuck right there. It's a vicious cycle for sure! And I can't understand why more people don't see and understand that that's how the game of life is 'played'. Maybe you will now that I've pointed it out to you. (Tapping my fingers on the table)

But, to be honest......I didn't get it either, until it just clicked one day. I'm sure glad they don't burn you at the stake anymore for your beliefs. They don't, do they?????? (GULP)

Manifesting is also about being in the right frequency to have our manifestations come to fruition. It's like wanting to hear Country Music that is on 101.5 but you have your radio set on 105.1. You aren't going to hear the station you want because you have tuned into another station (frequency). Or to a feeling - as it applies here.

Just think about that for a minute. The Country music station is still playing Country music all the time, whether or not you are tuned into it.

190 · SHIRLEY BRADY

But, if you are tuned into a head-banger or Soft Rock music station, you won't be hearing any Country music. NEVAH! You could WANT to hear Country music all day long and never hear it unless you TUNE INTO IT! This must be easy to understand. Isn't it? (tap, tap…is this Mic on?)

CHAPTER 24

The End? Or The And?

So I come to the last chapter of my book, and also of my life – uhhhh I mean this life. But it doesn't feel like the end yet because there are still many more things I want to learn, and still many more people I have yet to meet and learn from. And maybe some who will take away a lesson or two from what I have to share as well.

But I sense that I will continue learning and sharing in my next life, on that Storyboard too. So maybe you and I will meet again. You see, eternity is a really, really loooong time.

I hope the bits and pieces of my life that I've shared have allowed you to know me a little better, or at least understand a little better about what and why I believe the way that I do.

We all have life experiences that result in what makes us 'tick'. I hope that by sharing mine, it will give some insight into what possibly makes you tick too – and awaken you to reasons you may not have even thought of before.

Some will learn a little more.....a little faster.....and a little deeper on this journey; but the lessons are all there for anyone to learn them. And no one is actually 'left behind'. We will all learn our lessons when it's the exact right time to learn them. As the saying goes, "When the student is ready, the teacher will appear."

We all have different lessons that are meant distinctly for each of us. But I think the supreme message for everyone is to always be kind and to love one another. This allows us to be loved by others as well. If we always start with kindness and love, every other action can't help but be better from that starting point. And we can either learn our lessons through fear or through love. I choose love.

If we concentrate on our own journey and allow everyone else to concentrate on theirs, life will be much more enjoyable for everyone.

And it's ok that we don't want to associate with everyone in the same way. Those who we don't 'click' with, just aren't supposed to be part of our particular tribe. Everyone matters, but those who we feel closest to have a deeper purpose for being part of our relationship.

I hope those who may need it most, understand the fundamental meaning of, "What other people think of us is none of our business". We don't have to twist and turn our lives inside out to make others feel better. Or to like us either. Allowing is the first step. And allowing others to make their own way as we make ours is the next step. And then it can be Zip-a-dee-doo-dah, zip-a-dee-ay – my, oh my, what a wonderful day from then on.

And you will probably encounter some 'brats' in your life too. Brats (or bully's) are many times young teens who think they know everything and are just plain rude. I worked with one of those types recently at my last job. She is what is known as a 'mean girl'.

It was obvious that she had never, or rarely ever been told 'no'. She was just not a very nice person. She would talk about all of the other employees and the owner to me, and as she did, she was telling me, 'don't say anything....but'. And that's the biggest clue that she was definitely talking about me too when I wasn't around.

But if you live your life in the way that anyone who really matters won't believe falsehoods about you anyway, then you have nothing to worry about. And those who do believe unkind rumors about you were never the type of 'friends' worth having.

So, when someone shows you that they would rather believe a rumor about you, without being adult enough to ask you about the rumor first, it tells you much more about that person than words could ever say. You must be aware that they are merely trying to stay in the group where their type of behavior feels most comfortable. A group you wouldn't want to be part of.

But this girl's young age didn't account for the fact that this wasn't my first experience with this tactic, and I could read right through her. Or that my Mom had taught me about that kind of behavior when I was just a kid myself! But there are also grown-ups who act this way as well. And I use the term 'grown-ups' loosely, because people who behave this way have really never actually matured at all.

The funny thing is that we end up blaming the teenage bully for their behavior when it's actually the parents we should be taking umbrage with for not teaching their children how to be good people. But their parents are very likely the same way. You know the saying, 'The apple doesn't fall far from the tree!'

I do feel that we run into those types of people in life so that we can appreciate the ones who have been taught to be polite and ARE nice. Contrasts in life are what allow us to learn and expand our perspectives. Because every encounter we have can teach us something of value.

And that goes for people who disagree with you on religion, politics or other beliefs you have. If they unfriend you or distance themselves from you because you don't or won't believe as they do, then they also weren't very good friends! And I say, "Bye, Felicia".

And don't worry about those who say they don't want to hear all your inspirational mumbo-jumbo either. It just isn't their time to 'get it'. Don't be offended. Live your own truth and realize that they just don't feel very comfortable with anything inspirational. It isn't who they are.

Remember that misery loves company, water seeks its own level, and birds of a feather flock together. These sayings don't have longevity for no reason at all. So stay in your own lane, with your own flock and always with the highest amount of positive vibrations that you can muster, and you will be just fine. Don't get down in the dregs with anyone. That reminds me of another one – 'When you lie down with dogs, you get fleas'.

My Mom taught me those things when I was just a little girl. And I've learned that you were right about a lot of things that you told me MOM! And I did listen. LOL

I've observed that most people are always looking for the Happy Endings in life. Don't get me wrong, I love a happy ending as much as anyone. But I think we are missing out on a lot of happiness when we don't notice all the Happy Beginnings and the Happy Middles of life as well.

A life that is compassionate and loving is the best way to live if you want to leave the kind of legacy that will matter. If you only care about yourself, then good luck with that. What you put out into the Universe is exactly what will come back to you. It IS your choice. But I would caution you to choose wisely. We can either build a life of love, compassion and serenity......or build our own prison.

One day I will die too. And all the things that I thought were so important won't be important for me anymore. All of my 'things' will be left for my loved ones to sort out and decide what to do with.

The only thing that will matter is that I will be missed. And I hope that will be the case. And isn't being missed much better than a 'good riddance' anytime? I do know that I won't ever have any regrets about the time I spent with loved ones and good friends.

My perspective is sharper and much different now than what it was in my youth. The saying that hindsight is 20/20 is very true. I can now better understand the 20-year-old me and the 30 and 40 and 50 and 60-year-old me, and my approaching 70's more clearly. And now all of my decades make more sense to me. I can see the whole picture of Shirley's life and make sense of how and why it unfolded as it did.

Do I wish I had this clarity while I was living all of my years? Hell yeah! But that isn't how it works. I don't really know how I made it through all the losses I had to bear in life at the time I was going through it, because I didn't have the clarity I do now. But I also think that those very losses are what allowed me to awaken in my awareness of what life is all about. And in essence, to be able to appreciate life even more.

I've learned not to sweat the small stuff. And it's all small stuff in the grand scheme of life!

Would it have been easier if I had known what I know now about why my journey was taking me down each path? Heck yeah! But knowing that I did make it through, allows me to not be as fearful of my path going forward. Now if anyone says to Go To Hell....I can tell them that I've already been there and whatever they are offering, is definitely not even close to the Hell I've known.

Little Shirley Recchia has had quite a ride on the roller coaster of life. The physical-life Shirley would have been very frightened if she had known all that lay before her ahead of time. That's where the veil comes in handy. But she would have loved hearing about all of the wonderful people who would appear in her life too.

The contrasts of life balance out most of the time. Not always, but if we focus mostly on the happy times, it does help us to bear the sadness a little more easily.

I've often been told that I am wise, but I would bet that not many would trade me for my wisdom if they had to experience all that I have, to have gained that wisdom.

Wisdom is really insight. And insight comes from understanding. And understanding can only come from experience. And our experiences include the happy and the sad.

The secret to 'making it through' the rough patches in life is to stay kind and not blame anyone for anything that has happened in your life. Bitterness is a dangerous pill to swallow. As the saying goes, "Bitterness is like drinking poison and expecting the other person to die."

Bitterness, resentment, and anger will only hurt the person who is consumed by it. The operative word being 'consumed'.

And I have often thought that although the pain of loss is so deep and painful, I wouldn't trade having my loved ones in my life for the time we were allotted, even if I did have to suffer so much from the loss of them.

Many times wisdom is merely accepting that you don't know everything. And that it's OK not to know everything. And it's OK that not everyone likes us either because when we are completely honest, we know that we don't like everyone the same either. We all feel most comfortable in our own circles. And we are only able to see, feel, and think at the level of understanding that we have at any certain point in our life.

Also, we must not cast judgment about other peoples' tribes, because this means that we are also moving away from Divine Love. Further away from the Love that we ARE! This is why we feel so bad when we aren't demonstrating positive and loving behavior.

There are many 'souvenirs' from my life that I have picked up along my journey. Sorrow, pain, loss, misery, and heartache are the ones that hurt the most. My wish for you is that any wisdom that you will gain is only through the most pleasant life situations possible and that you have much to be grateful for. But that's going to be up to you.

And I have many beautiful souvenirs that I cherish as well: Joy, wonderful friendships, lasting relationships, two marriages with amazing men, and three of the most wonderful children that anyone could ever be blessed with, and a stepson that we made many special memories with. And the grandchildren have been the icing on the cake of life for me.

I must say that I was very fortunate in the in-law department as well. Both of my mother/father-in-law(s) were great to me. Terry's mom and dad and I may have gotten off to a bit of a rocky start because they didn't want Terry to marry so young, but everything was fine after the fact. Marilyn did tell me many times through the years how sorry she was and how happy she was that I was in their family.

Mike's mom and dad were the best parents anyone could ever ask for. Their given names were Mary Anne and Billy, but everyone called them Nana and Granddaddy. There isn't a day that goes by that Mike doesn't say how much he misses his parents. I don't think many of us appreciate our parents as much as we should while we have them with us. And when they are gone....it's too late.

We all must bear the sad times as well as the pleasures of life because without everything in the mix, life would just be a tasteless broth. And how wonderfully blessed is it to have had so many loved ones in life that it will break your heart to say goodbye to them? And them to you.

I pray that the rest of my journey is smooth-going and that there will be no more painful losses. But, in addition to understanding that whatever unfolds in our life is unfolding exactly as it should – my physical self is also a realist who understands that nothing is promised. So I will continue to savor and appreciate every sweet second that I am given in this 'Experiment' called Life.

Everyone has a story and not everyone will always understand your story. Just as we cannot always understand everyone else's story. But the point of our life is to learn our own lessons.

Life is made up of EACH of our stories. Allowing someone else to tell you how to live your life just doesn't make good sense, does it? Not even if it's your spouse or your children. It's the ultimate waste of your very own life to let someone else hold the 'keys'. Doesn't it really seem counter-productive to try to live any story that wasn't meant for you! It's like wearing a shoe that is not your size. It will become very uncomfortable after a while. Not to mention the 'blisters'!

If I could give one piece of advice to anyone reading this, it would be to PAY ATTENTION!!! When we pay attention, everything becomes much clearer. When we pay attention, we can understand other people's perspectives better, or at least maybe understand a little more clearly how they got to their point of view. And another reason to pay close attention to life is that there are clues everywhere, guiding us to our most perfect existence.

It reminds me of the Invisible Gorilla video. That video is an experiment that shows people who are dressed in either a black shirt or a white shirt and they are throwing around a basketball. The narrator tells you to count how many times the people in the white shirts pass the ball to the other players in the black shirts.

What happens is that while you are viewing the video and trying to focus on how many times the white-shirted people pass the ball, a gorilla comes into the mix and one of the people in the black shirt leaves the group. And the curtain behind the players also changes color. Most people don't notice those changes. This experiment shows that when we focus too much on things that may not matter, or we are focusing on some things too intently because we are worried about something, or trying to keep track, we miss so many other things that are happening right in front of our eyes.

Another example of not seeing the forest for the trees analogy is, how many times have you been looking for your glasses, only to realize that they are on your head? Or have you ever been ON YOUR CELL PHONE and think that you forgot where you put your cell phone and start looking for it? These are examples of panicking or worrying about something so intently, that you don't even realize that you already have it.

It's those very times that we don't pay attention to our instincts that we veer off center. It's those times that we don't pay attention that our marriages, or our friendships, or our closeness in our relationships, and even with our children that we miss out on most.

When we do pay attention, life goes along much more effortlessly. When we pay attention, we notice when we are going against the stream of life, instead of going with the flow. When we pay attention, we notice all that we have to be grateful for, instead of worrying about what our neighbors may have. Just paying attention can be one of the best things we can do for ourselves, and for everyone we come in contact with.

This beautiful thing called Life can seem so very complicated. But only because we make it so. Life is actually a gift that is meant to be JOY-ful and for us to en-JOY. But we allow our ego minds to mess with perfection time and time again. It really doesn't have to be difficult at all.

If we could just learn to relax and allow the flow of life to unfold, we would find that God/The Universe/The All That Is…..is much better at planning, than we ever could be. Higher Source has GOT THIS! So stop trying to be the one controlling everything. It's being just a tad egotistical to believe we could do it better, don't ya' think?

Our ego mind tells us that we are not enough just as we are. It tells us that we must always be doing better than our neighbor(s). It makes us feel less than if we aren't out-doing other people. It makes us feel that 'we' are inferior to 'them'. It makes us care too much about the opinion of others. Feeling whole tells us that we don't need to compare ourselves to anyone else because we are sure of our own self-worth.

The ego-mind is always trying to enhance itself by outside approval. Being egocentric means being centered in the self.

This isn't to say that we have to do away with our ego, because that is not possible. It just means that we can tame it, and we don't have to believe everything that it's telling us in our monkey-mind yakking that is always going on in our head.

So feel whole Peeps! Because you are. Feel the JOY in feeling that you are perfectly who you are meant to be along your life's journey. Stop trying to control everything and accept that what is happening in life is here for us to learn and to grow from. Everything may not always be rainbows and lollipops, but we can be better people from learning the lessons that come to us.....and we will grow stronger and feel secure in knowing that everything will be alright in the end.

The Woo-Woo in me begs to convey that we did call to us whatever is happening in our lives FOR us, not TO us. When you begin to understand this, life will be less confusing and you will look for the lessons in everything, because you will see it as fulfilling your soul's journey, instead of damning it.

And as for any future monetary wealth that I may or not attain in this lifetime – I can say without a doubt that I feel like the richest woman in the world for so many reasons. I can now understand the whys and why not's of my life so much more clearly than I ever did before I 'awakened' through the Grace of The All That Is.

And I wish the same for all of you. May your Blessings abound and you recognize each and every one of them when they do show up for you.

I hope you have enjoyed reading my book as much as I have enjoyed writing it. If you would like to keep up with me, you can find me at:

Facebook: https://www.facebook.com/shirleybradyfl

Twitter: https://twitter.com/Gommyatthebeach

Blog: http://gommysgoodies.blogspot.com

Smashwords Interview:
https://www.smashwords.com/interview/Gommy

Smashwords profile page:
https://www.smashwords.com/profile/view/Gommy

You can also let me know if you would be interested in reading more about my spiritual beliefs, or just say hi on any of these sites!

Hugs and Mush, Gommy

Made in the
USA
Columbia, SC